Telecollaboration and virtual exchange across disciplines: in service of social inclusion and global citizenship

Edited by Anna Turula, Malgorzata Kurek, and Tim Lewis

Published by Research-publishing.net, a not-for-profit association
Voillans, France, info@research-publishing.net

© 2019 by Editors (collective work)
© 2019 by Authors (individual work)

Telecollaboration and virtual exchange across disciplines: in service of social inclusion and global citizenship
Edited by Anna Turula, Malgorzata Kurek, and Tim Lewis

Publication date: 2019/07/02

Rights: the whole volume is published under the Attribution-NonCommercial-NoDerivatives International (CC BY-NC-ND) licence; **individual articles may have a different licence**. Under the CC BY-NC-ND licence, the volume is freely available online (https://doi.org/10.14705/rpnet.2019.35.9782490057429) for anybody to read, download, copy, and redistribute provided that the author(s), editorial team, and publisher are properly cited. Commercial use and derivative works are, however, not permitted.

Disclaimer: Research-publishing.net does not take any responsibility for the content of the pages written by the authors of this book. The authors have recognised that the work described was not published before, or that it was not under consideration for publication elsewhere. While the information in this book is believed to be true and accurate on the date of its going to press, neither the editorial team nor the publisher can accept any legal responsibility for any errors or omissions. The publisher makes no warranty, expressed or implied, with respect to the material contained herein. While Research-publishing.net is committed to publishing works of integrity, the words are the authors' alone.

Trademark notice: product or corporate names may be trademarks or registered trademarks, and are used only for identification and explanation without intent to infringe.

Copyrighted material: every effort has been made by the editorial team to trace copyright holders and to obtain their permission for the use of copyrighted material in this book. In the event of errors or omissions, please notify the publisher of any corrections that will need to be incorporated in future editions of this book.

Typeset by Research-publishing.net
Cover illustration by © Julien Eichinger - Adobe Stock.com
Cover design by © Raphaël Savina (raphael@savina.net)

ISBN13: 978-2-490057-42-9 (Ebook, PDF, colour)
ISBN13: 978-2-490057-43-6 (Ebook, EPUB, colour)
ISBN13: 978-2-490057-41-2 (Paperback - Print on demand, black and white)
Print on demand technology is a high-quality, innovative and ecological printing method; with which the book is never 'out of stock' or 'out of print'.

British Library Cataloguing-in-Publication Data.
A cataloguing record for this book is available from the British Library.

Legal deposit, UK: British Library.
Legal deposit, France: Bibliothèque Nationale de France - Dépôt légal: juillet 2019.

Table of contents

v   Notes on contributors

1   Introduction
Anna Turula, Malgorzata Kurek, and Tim Lewis

7   When more is less: unexpected challenges and benefits of telecollaboration
Daniela Caluianu

15   Mainstreaming virtual mobility – helping teachers to get onboard
Alastair Creelman and Corina Löwe

23   From 'CoCo' to 'FloCoCo': the evolving role of virtual exchange (practice report)
Régine Barbier and Elizabeth Benjamin

31   Challenges of the transatlantic cross-disciplinary ENVOIE-UFRUG project
Juan Albá Duran and Gerdientje Oggel

41   Virtual School Garden Exchange – thinking globally, gardening locally
Johanna Lochner

49   'FORE - UEK Telecollaboration 2017' – virtual exchange in business studies
Małgorzata Marchewka and Reeta Raina

57   When two worldviews meet: promoting mutual understanding between 'secular' and religious students of Islamic studies in Russia and the United States
Alexander Knysh, Anna Matochkina, Daria Ulanova, Philomena Meechan, and Todd Austin

65   Gamifying intercultural telecollaboration tasks for pre-mobility students
Marta Giralt and Liam Murray

73   A discussion on how teachers assess what foreign language students learn in telecollaboration
Suzi Marques Spatti Cavalari

Table of contents

81 The Global Virtual Teams Project: learning to manage team dynamics in virtual exchange
Rachel Lindner and Dónal O'Brien

91 Virtual exchange across disciplines: telecollaboration and the question of asymmetrical task design
Martin Štefl

99 A proposal to study the links between the sociocultural and the linguistic dimensions of eTandem interactions
Marco Cappellini

105 Lived experience of connected practice: Clavier
Teresa Mackinnon

111 Vocabulary learning in Mandarin Chinese – German eTandems
Julia Renner

119 Author index

Notes on contributors

1. Editors

Anna Turula is an experienced CALL/EFL teacher and teacher trainer. She is currently based at the Pedagogical University in Krakow, Poland, where she is Head of the Technology Enhanced Language Education Department. Her research interests include new technologies in language learning and teacher training, cognitive and affective factors in CALL, and e-classroom dynamics. She is the proponent and organiser of the PL-CALL conference (2013, 2014, 2016, in Warsaw and Krakow) and the editor of the Peter Lang series *Studies in Computer Assisted Language Learning*.

Malgorzata Kurek is Researcher and Lecturer at the Institute of Foreign Languages, Jan Dlugosz University, Częstochowa, Poland. She holds a PhD in applied linguistics and works as Assistant Professor and TEFL Trainer long involved in academic-level virtual exchange. Her principal research addresses the issues of CALL, teacher education, task design, and digital literacy. She is currently Training Officer for Unicollaboration and Co-Designer of several virtual exchange training programmes.

Dr Tim Lewis is Senior Lecturer (Languages) at the Open University, UK, where he has worked since 2002. From 2013-2017, Tim acted as Director of Postgraduate Studies in the Centre for Research in Education and Educational Technology. Tim's publications include: *Autonomous Language Learning in Tandem* (Sheffield: Academy Electronic Press, 2003), *Language Learning Strategies in Independent Settings* (Clevedon: Multilingual Matters, 2008), *Online Intercultural Exchange: Policy, Pedagogy, Practice* (New York: Routledge, 2016), and *Learner Autonomy and Web 2.0* (Sheffield : Equinox, 2017).

2. Reviewers

Sarah Guth is the president of UNICollaboration, a cross-disciplinary organisation for telecollaboration and virtual exchange in higher education and teaches English as a foreign language at the University of Padova, Italy. She was the Programme Coordinator at the SUNY COIL Centre and designed their Professional Development Programme. Her research focusses on intercultural communication and the normalisation of virtual exchange in higher education. She is the project manager for UNICollaboration's participation in the consortium that is leading the European Commission's pilot project; Erasmus+ Virtual Exchange.

Andreas Müller-Hartmann is Professor of Teaching English as a Foreign Language (TEFL) and the Head of the English Department at the Pädagogische Hochschule, Heidelberg, Germany. He holds a PhD in American Studies from the University of Osnabrück, Germany. His research interests include task-supported language learning, the use of technology in the EFL classroom, the development of intercultural communicative competence, and teacher education. He has co-written books on TEFL in the secondary classroom (2004, 2009) and task-supported language learning (2011 and 2013, with Marita Schocker). He has co-edited books on qualitative research in foreign language learning and teaching (2001) and task-based language learning with technology (2008). He teaches TEFL, TSLL, CALL, and American cultural studies.

Robert O'Dowd is Associate Professor for English as a Foreign Language and Applied Linguistics at the University of León, Spain. He has taught at universities in Ireland, Germany, and Spain and has over 40 publications on the application of virtual exchange in university and pre-university education settings. One of his most recent books is the co-edited volume Online Intercultural Exchange: Policy, Pedagogy, Practice, for Routledge. He was the founding president of the UNICollaboration academic organisation for telecollaboration and virtual exchange (www.unicollaboration.org). He has been invited to be plenary speaker at international conferences in the US, Asia, and across Europe, and he is co-editor of the Peter Lang book series Telecollaboration in Education. He was recently invited to be co-editor for a special edition of the prestigious journal Language Learning & Technology on Virtual Exchange in foreign language education.

H. Müge Satar, PhD, is Lecturer in Applied Linguistics and TESOL at Newcastle University. Her research interests are in the areas of language learning and teaching, especially in multimodal computer-mediated communication via videoconferencing, TBLT, and social presence. In her research, she uses both quantitative and qualitative methods, such as social semiotics, interactional linguistics, and social network analysis. She has publications in Language Learning & Technology, the Modern Language Journal, ReCALL, and CALICO.

Shannon Sauro is Associate Professor in the Department of Culture, Languages, and Media at Malmö University, Sweden. Her research explores language learning in the digital wilds, particularly in fan communities, and its relevance for the language classroom. She is co-editor, with Carol A. Chapelle, of The handbook of technology and second language teaching and learning, with Joanna Pitura of CALL for mobility, and with Katerina Zourou of the special issue of Language Learning & Technology on CALL in the Digital Wilds.

Carine Ullom, EdD, is Associate Dean of Instructional Innovation at Ottawa University in Ottawa, KS. She holds undergraduate degrees in computer science and German, an MA in German Languages and Literatures, and an EdD in Educational Leadership. Ullom received a Fulbright grant to study computer assisted language learning at Oldenburg Universität in Germany. She has over 20 years' experience with implementing educational technology in higher education and has designed and co-taught several Globally Connected Teaching and Learning (GCTL) courses. Her research focusses on the role of GCTL in supporting intercultural competence development among undergraduate students.

3. Authors

Todd Austin leads the Videoconferencing Group at the University of Michigan's College of Literature, Science, and the Arts. He has worked on the design and implementation of virtual exchange classes since 2009. In that time, he has

Notes on contributors

connected courses on a broad range of subjects with partners in Russia, Germany, Haiti, Brazil, Japan, India, Israel, Egypt, South Africa, and many others. Todd's academic background is in Russian politics and astrophysics and he holds a BA from the University of Rochester.

Régine Barbier (Professeur agrégé d'anglais, Strasbourg University) is a lecturer in English, in charge of work placements and international relations in the department of Networks and Telecommunications, Colmar University Institute of Technology, Université de Haute-Alsace. She loves teaching, IT, languages, and traveling, and encourages students to do their internships abroad. She believes virtual exchange is a wonderful opportunity for students to improve language skills and enhance intercultural awareness, and enjoys collaborating with partners abroad and participating in international conferences.

Elizabeth Benjamin is Lecturer in French at Coventry University. Her research interests intersect visual culture, comparative aesthetics, and cultural memory. Her current work explores the role of memorialisation in the formation of national identity. Other research interests include: links between music, writing, and art; comic books; archiving and silent films; economies of visual art; and the role of monuments and city spaces for cultural memory. She is the author of Dada and Existentialism: the Authenticity of Ambiguity (Palgrave Macmillan 2016).

Juan Albá Duran is Lecturer of Spanish Proficiency at the University of Groningen (The Netherlands), where he currently holds the position of coordinator of Spanish Language Learning and where he has developed virtual exchange projects with the University of Barcelona (Spain) and the University of La Frontera (Chile). He is also Teacher-Researcher in the European funded project EVOLVE, which aims to mainstream virtual exchange and provide evidence of its impact at student, teacher, and institutional levels.

Daniela Caluianu is Professor of English Language and Linguistics at Otaru University of Commerce, Japan. Her research interests include lexical semantics, construction grammar, typology, and EFL. A few years ago, she thought she had invented a new teaching method only to discover that it had been around for a long time and that it had a name – telecollaboration. Ever since, she has been trying to help colleagues avoid her mistake.

Marco Cappellini is Assistant Professor (Maître de Conférences) in didactics of foreign languages and cultures at Aix-Marseille University and a member of the Speech and Language Laboratory (Laboratoire Parole & Langage UMR 7309). His main areas of research are the use of computer-mediated communication for foreign language teaching-learning, telecollaboration, tandem language learning, learner autonomy, and teacher education.

Suzi Marques Spatti Cavalari is Assistant Professor of English as a Foreign Language at the Department of Modern Languages of São Paulo State University (UNESP) – São José do Rio Preto. She holds an MA and PhD in Applied Linguistics and her research interests lie in telecollaborative learning, assessment, autonomy, and normalisation of telecollaboration across the curriculum.

Alastair Creelman is e-learning Specialist in the section for Higher Education Development at Linnaeus University, Sweden. His focus areas are open education, MOOCs, social media in education, and virtual mobility, and he has been involved in several national and international projects in these areas. He is an EDEN Fellow and was a member of the committee that developed the new ISO 21001 standard Management System for Educational Organisations.

Marta Giralt (MA, M.Phil, PhD) is Lecturer in Applied Linguistics and Spanish at University of Limerick since 2015. She teaches ICT and languages, intercultural communication, foreign language teaching and Spanish. Her research interests are in applied linguistics, in particular, second language acquisition and oral language, ICT, and language learning and intercultural communication. In 2007 she was awarded with first prize in the II Premio Cristobal de Villalón for Pedagogic Innovation at Universidad de Valladolid, Spain. She has participated in several projects involving ICT, SLA, and FLT and currently is a national representative for the Cost Action EnetCollect (European

Notes on contributors

Network for Combining Language Learning with Crowdsourcing Techniques). A list of recent publications are available here: https://ulsites.ul.ie/mlal/dr-marta-giralt-0

Alexander Knysh is Professor of Islamic Studies at the University of Michigan and Principal Investigator at the St. Petersburg State University, Russia. His research interests include Islamic Mysticism (Sufism), Qur'anic Studies, history of Muslim theological, philosophical, and juridical thought, and Islamic/Islamist movements in comparative perspectives. He has numerous academic publications on these subjects, including ten books. He is Section Editor of *Encyclopedia of Islam* and Executive Editor of *Handbook Series of Sufi Studies* published by E.J. Brill, Leiden, and Boston.

Rachel Lindner teaches English and coordinates the language division of the International Business Studies programme at the University of Paderborn. The main focus of her work is in ESAP. Her special interests are in multiliteracies practice in ESAP, intercultural learning, and in teaching language with educational technology.

Johanna Lochner is Doctoral Student at Humboldt, Universität zu Berlin in Germany. Her research interest is on Virtual School Garden Exchange in primary and secondary schools and the framework of Education for Sustainable Development (ESD). She co-coordinates the working group "Go! Global" of the ESD Expert Net – a virtual school exchange programme linking local actions related to the Sustainable Development Goals globally. Find out more: https://www.agrar.hu-berlin.de/en/institut-en/departments/daoe/didactics-agri-horticulture/staff/JL?set_language=en and http://www.esd-expert.net/go-global-virtual-school-exchange.html.

Corina Löwe is Assistant Professor in German Language and Literature at the Language Department of Linnaeus University, Sweden. Between 2015-2017, she was Head of the Global Classroom project. Together with Alastair Creelman, she is currently working on the Erasmus+ project Moonlite, which aims to promote academic education with MOOCs.

Teresa Mackinnon is an award winning language teacher and Certified Member of the Association for Learning Technology. She is experienced in technology enhanced learning design in secondary and higher education. She curates CPD resources for language tutors and is active on twitter as @warwicklanguage. She researches and designs to find solutions supporting student-centred pedagogy. An active advocate of computer-mediated communication and open educational practice, she is currently involved in the EVOLVE project supporting the mainstreaming of virtual exchange.

Małgorzata Marchewka is Research and Teaching Assistant at the Management Process Department (Faculty of Management) at Cracow University of Economics (Poland). In 2009 she graduated from Applied Psychology (Jagiellonian University) and from Management (Cracow University of Economics, major in Controlling and financial management). Her research interests regard problems of cross-cultural communication, negotiations, and behavioural problems of management.

Anna Matochkina, Senior Lecturer at the Department of Oriental Philosophy and Cultural Science, Institute of Philosophy, St. Petersburg State University. Since completing her dissertation on "Religion and Power in the Doctrine of Ibn Taymiyya", Anna has served as Senior Lecturer at the Department of Oriental Philosophy and Cultural Studies. Her research interests include Arab-Muslim culture, Arab-Muslim philosophy, Arab-Muslim art, Islamic fundamentalism, the life and works of Ibn Taymiyyah, the History of Islam in Russia, Arabic graffiti, and orientalism in St. Petersburg's architecture. Since 2014, she has been a project participant in the Research Laboratory for Analysis and Modeling of Social Processes. Political Islam/Islamism: Theory and Practice in Comparative and Historical Perspective.

Philomena Meechan is Instructional Learning Lead at the Language Resource Centre, College of Literature, Science, and the Arts, University of Michigan. Philomena works with faculty to integrate instructional technology into foreign language, literature, and culture courses. She has been involved in designing and supporting virtual international exchanges since 2000 and currently co-

Notes on contributors

coordinates a grant project at the University of Michigan to foster such exchanges in a variety of disciplines. She has an MA in Romance Linguistics (Spanish) from the University of Michigan.

Dr Liam Murray is Senior Lecturer in French and Language Technologies in the School of Modern Languages and Applied Linguistics at the University of Limerick, Ireland and teaches courses on CALL, digital games-based language learning, French civilization and media, cyberculture, e-learning, and evaluation at both undergraduate and postgraduate levels. Areas of research interest include CALL, games-based learning, and the application of social media and blog writing to second language acquisition. He is a reviewer for a number of international research journals. Since 1991, he has contributed many articles and book chapters on these research areas, being published in journals such as AJET, System, Eludamos, Journal for Computer Game Culture, Classroom Discourse, Educational Media International, ReCall, and Learning, Media and Technology. Academic homepage: http://www3.ul.ie/llcc/liam-murray/

Dr Dónal O'Brien is Lecturer and Researcher in Strategy and International Management in the Technological University Dublin. He completed his PhD on the strategic activities of managers operating in multinational enterprises. Dr O'Brien's PhD was recognised by the Academy of International Business (AIB) – UK & Ireland chapter conference with the Neil Hood and Stephen Young Prize for the Most Original New Work and the Irish Academy of Management annual conference as the Best Postgraduate Paper. This has led on to his major research interests in the areas of the microfoundations of subsidiary initiative, subsidiary management, entrepreneurship, global virtual teams, and managing coopetition.

Gerdientje Oggel is Lecturer of Spanish Proficiency and physical mobility coordinator at the Department of European Languages and Cultures of the University of Groningen (The Netherlands). Currently she is also a teacher/researcher of the European Funded EVOLVE project which seeks to mainstream virtual exchange across disciplines in institutes of higher education. Since 2011, she has been involved in several telecollaboration projects focussing on the development of linguistic, intercultural, and digital skills.

Reeta Raina is Professor and Chairperson of Communication Area at FORE School of Management (India) and has more than 32 years of academic, research, and training experience in premier national institutions. Her areas of interests are: organisational communication, employee engagement, work engagement, non-verbal communication, and listening skills. She has a research book to her credit titled "The Constitutive role of Communication in Building Effective Organizations" published by LAMBERT, and she has been awarded many prizes at international conferences and the Best Professor award in HRM.

Julia Renner holds an BA/MA in Chinese Studies from the University of Vienna. She has been granted a PhD scholarship by the Austrian Academy of Sciences and is currently pursuing her PhD in linguistics at the University of Vienna. Her research focusses on teaching and learning Chinese as a foreign language and technology enhanced language learning.

Martin Štefl is a full time member of the department of language studies of MIAS School of Business, Czech Technical University in Prague. Martin teaches both undergraduate and graduate BE courses in English and German, focussing on skills training, in particular on the use telecollaborative practices; he is professionally interested in philosophy and business ethics and researches into critical thinking and its applications in language teaching.

Daria Ulanova, PhD, is Assistant Lecturer of the Faculty of Asian and African Studies, Department of Arabic Philology, St. Petersburg State University. Daria's PhD thesis is "Fatwas as the source of Islamic family law in the Ottoman Empire late XV-early XVII centuries". Her academic interests include history of law in the Ottoman Empire; features of the Ottoman legal system; coexistence of the two legal systems in the Ottoman Empire (state and religious); Islamic family law in the Ottoman Empire in the XV-XVII centuries; and family law in the modern Turkish Republic. She has publications concerning the subjects above. She is also a current participant of Research Laboratory for Analysis and Modeling of Social Processes at St. Petersburg State University.

Introduction

Anna Turula[1], Malgorzata Kurek[2], and Tim Lewis[3]

The following collection of short papers is an outcome of the Third Conference on Telecollaboration in Higher Education hosted by Pedagogical University in Krakow, Poland, from the 25th to the 27th of April 2018. After the two previous editions of the conference, the first one held in Leon in 2014 and the second in Dublin in 2016, we have been offered another opportunity to gain an insight into the current state of telecollaboration, aka Virtual Exchange (VE), a rapidly developing form of learning which engages students from geographically and culturally distinct academic institutions in meaningful computer-mediated tasks.

The conference took as its main theme the role of telecollaboration and VE in service of social inclusion and global citizenship, and pointed to the learning potential of VE across academic disciplines. It attracted as many as 154 novice and experienced VE researchers and practitioners from 27 countries. As always, it was extremely inspiring and thought-provoking to join this vibrant community of colleagues from all over the world and share their excitement for VE during academic and social encounters. While the former assured high quality research input, the latter helped the participants expand their social networks and form new partnerships – the very essence of VE projects.

The conference provided space for highly varied research and practice presentations, with three outstanding and inspiring keynote-speeches by professors Steve Thorne, Barbara Lewandowska Tomaszczyk, and Francesca Helm. Following the theme of the conference and based on the major conference

---

1. Pedagogical University of Krakow, Krakow, Poland; anna.turula@up.krakow.pl; https://orcid.org/0000-0003-3086-8591

2. Jan Dlugosz University, Czestochowa, Poland; gkurka@gmail.com; https://orcid.org/0000-0002-7191-6273

3. The Open University, Milton Keynes, England; timothy.lewis@open.ac.uk

How to cite: Turula, A., Kurek, M., & Lewis, T. (2019). Introduction. In A. Turula, M. Kurek & T. Lewis (Eds), *Telecollaboration and virtual exchange across disciplines: in service of social inclusion and global citizenship* (pp. 1-6). Research-publishing.net. https://doi.org/10.14705/rpnet.2019.35.933

strands, the papers collected in this volume offer theoretical and practical considerations on the most recent stage of development of VE. A number of papers describe specific VEs, reflecting on ways of improving them through modifications to task design, as well as through the use of different tools and techniques. Some of these chapters are practice reports offering invaluable insights into telecollaborative initiatives carried out over several years by experienced educators. The papers have been restricted in length to 2,000 words, which justifies their compact format. This limitation posed a significant challenge in terms of assuring both clarity and comprehensibility of contributions, and our appreciation for authors' attempts to meet both criteria is all the greater. It is also important to note that, as VE is increasingly used across various academic disciplines, a large group of chapter submissions reflect on the lessons learnt in the delivery of actual class-to-class exchanges.

In the first paper, **Daniela Caluianu** describes the evolution of a telecollaboration project between a Japanese university and a university in Romania. She focusses on the unexpected benefits and challenges emerging in VE projects and shows how adjusting task design to create space for reflection within the exchange can improve cross-cultural understanding and student self-awareness.

Alastair Creelman and **Corina Löwe** discuss an internal project at Linnaeus University, Sweden, whose aim is to facilitate international networking and online collaboration for the purpose of promoting virtual mobility. A special focus of the chapter is the careful selection of tools: in this case, a self-evaluation tool, enabling faculty to highlight potential development areas, as well a toolbox for digital collaboration. The authors emphasise the importance of mainstreaming VE in the process of internationalisation and highlight incentive-, strategy-, and culture-related factors as the main challenges that need to be overcome.

In their practice report, **Régine Barbier** and **Elizabeth Benjamin** present an online international learning exchange project involving students of French and International Relations at Coventry University and Networks and Telecommunications Engineering students at the Université de Haute- Alsace in

Colmar, France, which has been running since 2014. The chapter discusses the aims of the project, the impact of modifications made in its two recent iterations, as well as ways of providing the best VE experience to the participants.

Juan Albá Duran and **Gerdientje Oggel**'s chapter reports upon an exchange between Dutch students of Hispanic literature and a Chilean group enrolled in a course on journalism. Apart from discussing the challenges of an interdisciplinary telecollaborative project, the authors look at various contextual – socio-political, syllabus-related, and personal – constraints of the exchange and detail the lessons learnt from them. As they point out, the ability to deal with such constraints can be greatly increased if the instructors are prepared for them by adequate teacher training.

Johanna Lochner's chapter offers an overview of nine different virtual school garden exchange projects demonstrating how the global perspective of education for sustainable development can be integrated into primary education. Drawing on the data and experiences gathered in nine iterations of the project carried out within the span of 20 years, the author shows how digital media can be harnessed to make primary and secondary level learners explore various aspects of gardening.

On a more practical note, **Małgorzata Marchewka** and **Reeta Raina** describe how a large-scale VE between FORE School of Management, India, and Cracow University of Economics, Poland, helped enhance the understanding of managerial problems in modern business as well as facilitating cross-cultural communication, and developing positive attitudes to cooperation and sensitivity to cultural differences. The authors focus on the practical aspects of organising a large-scale VE project, including task design, the selection of tools, and the roles of teachers and their interventions.

Alexander Knysh, Anna Matochkina, Daria Ulanova, Philomena Meechan, and **Todd Austin** discuss results from two co-taught courses in Islamic studies shared as a VE between the University of Michigan, USA, and Saint Petersburg State University, Russia. They emphasise the uniqueness of the experience, which gave their students the opportunity to extend their language and communication skills as well as exposure to source material and educational approaches that they would have been otherwise unlikely to encounter.

Another group of chapters, while referring to actual VEs, place more stress on the authors' reflections on different aspects of telecollaboration and their importance to the success of the exchange.

In their chapter, **Marta Giralt** and **Liam Murray**, of the University of Limerick, argue that given appropriate task design and taking into account the specificity of the environment, preparatory pre-mobility telecollaborative exchanges can benefit from gamification to strengthen students' motivation to participate in such programmes.

A less common model of telecollaboration is presented by **Suzi Marques Spatti Cavalari** who provides insights into the Institutionally Integrated TeleTanDem programme, as practised at the Rio Preto campus of the Federal University of São Paulo, Brazil. In her contribution, the author discusses the role of feedback and offers a model of assessment practice implemented in an exchange of this kind.

Rachel Lindner and **Dónal O'Brien** explore the classroom/workplace connection, investigating the potential of telecollaboration in the business context. They argue that such projects can provide students with valuable pre-workplace experience giving them the skills needed to operate successfully in Global Virtual Teams – culturally, geographically, temporally, and functionally dispersed workgroups typical of the context they describe.

Martin Štefl zooms in on an experience with an asymmetric online intercultural exchange between three different groups of students of various business studies in Czechia, Hungary, and France. He observes that asymmetry can frequently be noted in different VEs and is not necessarily unwelcome, nor detrimental, to the aims of the telecollaboration.

Finally, a series of chapters explore innovative approaches to VE research methodology and, based on instructors' own experiences, propose innovative solutions in this area.

Marco Cappellini, of the Université d'Aix-Marseille, proposes a methodology for the empirical investigation of the link between the sociocultural and linguistic dimensions of interaction in eTandem via desktop videoconferencing. He shows how such a methodological framework can lead to intriguing and original research insights into telecollaboration.

Teresa Mackinnon, of Warwick University, offers insights into the data coming from auto ethnographic accounts of the participants of the Clavier Online Intercultural Exchange. She shows how the data were analysed using a grounded theory approach and analyses the discovery process undergone by the researcher, in interacting with the data, in her attempt to grapple with the complexity of the process.

Finally, **Julia Renner** of the University of Vienna, reports on a study of vocabulary learning in synchronous, multimodal eTandems focussing on Mandarin Chinese. The researcher adopts an emic, conversation analytic perspective and triangulates self-reported data from learner diaries with recordings of actual eTandem conversations.

As shown above, the papers published in the current collection offer insights into multiple aspects of VE, including design, implementation, and innovative research methodologies. The authors whose papers are collected here provide the reader with a broad sweep of perspectives on this complex, yet extremely stimulating learning environment, thus confirming the growing role and potential of VE in a wide range of higher education contexts.

As the editorial team, we are grateful to all the authors for sharing their inspiring contributions and do hope that their experiences will attract the attention of other academic researchers and educators at all levels to VE, inspiring them to

Introduction

embrace VE projects in an even wider range of disciplines and contexts. The open access accessibility of the current publication will hopefully assure this.

Last but not least, we would like to thank the team of reviewers who were kind enough to form our scientific committee for sharing their expertise in the process of scrutinizing all the papers. We also appreciate the incredibly smooth cooperation we have received from Research-publishing.net, whose publishing efficiency and professionalism added greatly to the current shape of this publication.

1. When more is less: unexpected challenges and benefits of telecollaboration

Daniela Caluianu[1]

Abstract

This article documents the changes undergone by a telecollaboration project between a Japanese university and a university in Romania. While the size of the project diminished with every passing year due to extrinsic and intrinsic causes, the quality of the exchanges improved. It became apparent that the main goals of the collaboration – improving cross-cultural understanding and increasing student self-awareness – were better served by reducing the number of tasks and allowing more time for reflection.

Keywords: cross-cultural understanding, self-awareness, institutional involvement, task.

1. Introduction

This article offers a candid account of three successive years of telecollaboration between Otaru University of Commerce, Japan (OUC), and Transilvania University of Brasov, Romania (TUB). After a promising start, the project – hailed by one of the first student participants as "a step towards the modern age in a bureaucratic university" and a "window to the world" – entered a process of reduction and simplification. This diminution was not due to loss of interest by the student participants or by the organizers, but by the overambitious structure of

---

1. Otaru University of Commerce, Otaru, Japan; daniela@res.otaru-uc.ac.jp

How to cite this chapter: Caluianu, D. (2019). When more is less: unexpected challenges and benefits of telecollaboration. In A. Turula, M. Kurek & T. Lewis (Eds), *Telecollaboration and virtual exchange across disciplines: in service of social inclusion and global citizenship* (pp. 7-13). Research-publishing.net. https://doi.org/10.14705/rpnet.2019.35.934

the project and by the asymmetrical burden it represented for the two institutions. Far from being detrimental to the project, the reduction proved beneficial in that it allowed more time for reflection and, thus, enhanced the cultural experience. This article will present the project, the factors that prompted the changes, and the lessons that can be drawn from this experience. Since the very small number of student participants makes it impossible to provide meaningful quantitative data, the article will focus on qualitative data: instructor observations and student testimony.

2. The project

The OUC-TUB project was initially designed around an OUC academic writing class and consisted of three units: (1) from presentation to essay, (2) from data collection to report, and (3) literature review. The course aimed to provide students with the tools needed for writing a graduation paper in English.

In the first year, virtual exchanges, both synchronous and asynchronous, took place at all stages throughout the three units. All the three types of interactions mentioned in O'Dowd and Ware (2009) were included: information exchange, comparison and analysis, and collaboration. In synchronous encounters, students watched each other's presentations and offered comments, together created survey questions, collected data, and discussed it, exchanged ideas on the article they had read, and reviewed each other's essays (for details see Caluianu, 2018).

In the second year of the partnership, the collaboration included only two units of the initial project and the Romanian students did not take part any longer in the essay writing activities. In the third year, the exchange was even more limited. It appears that, instead of growing, the project has been shrinking with every passing year. What prompted these changes?

The project was, from the start, modeled to answer the needs of the Japanese university. The telecollaboration was integrated with the OUC curriculum and was recognized as one of the main activities of a Blended-Learning Project (BLP) funded by the Japanese government. As such, it was scheduled in a time slot that would permit face-to-face communication with a European country, and it benefitted from technical support from the BLP staff.

The situation was very different for the Romanian university where the collaboration had no official status and was merely tolerated. The activities were piggybacked onto various classes during the first two years and carried out on a voluntary basis during students' free time in the third year. Faculty efforts were not rewarded in any way, a state of affairs that led to loss of interest by some of the participants.

Differences between partners in telecollaboration are not something uncommon. Rodas-Pérez, Villamediana-González, Chala, and Rico (2018) discuss a project that started with an asymmetric partnership, much like the one between OUC and TUB, but which managed to overcome the differences and ended up with a balanced relationship. The difference between that case and the one under discussion is the existence of an official relationship between the universities involved. Without the framework provided by an official inter-university agreement, the asymmetry between the two universities was difficult to resolve.

However, the main reason behind the gradual shrinking of the project was that the initial plan was too ambitious. The plan imposed a fast-paced rhythm and did not set aside time for reflection and for exploration. The students had to complete numerous tasks: making presentations, designing surveys, reading articles, writing essays, and providing peer reviews. This pace was accepted without complaint by the Japanese students but placed a heavy burden on the Romanian partners, who were used to a different workload in class, and contributed to their instructor's decision to quit the project. What is more, in this maelstrom of activities, there was little time left for dwelling on cultural differences or comparing communicative styles. This led to the need to eliminate some of the activities, which ended up adding depth to the collaboration.

Chapter 1

3. Discussion: changes and consequences

As mentioned above, the changes to the initial project were forced rather than implemented by choice, yet, once in place they proved advantageous. In the first year, the semester ended and, although the students were asked to reflect on their experience and give feedback through a questionnaire, there was no time left to discuss their answers and to analyze the experience. The student feedback, though positive, was vague. This is particularly true with respect to the central piece of the project: intercultural communication.

> "I think this class was more effective at the point of knowing different cultures and communicating with foreign people" (Year 1 Student 1, Caluianu, 2018, p. 62).

Several students mentioned 'knowing a different culture' as one of the best points of the class, yet it is unclear what that means and if it was more than an attempt to give the expected response.

The second year activities were more one-sided and offered less time for interaction. At the same time, by reducing the number of activities, it became possible to take more time for reflection. The Japanese students were asked to write an essay at the end of the semester, discussing the value of telecollaboration as a teaching instrument in the context of Japanese education. The essays offered an interesting culturally situated assessment of telecollaboration, but also some unexpected critical reactions: they articulated clearly their need for pre-exchange cultural training and for a more evenly-paced rhythm. The essays offered an insight into students' understanding of their place in the world and showed a higher degree of self-awareness than expected:

> "One of [the] barriers to practical telecollaboration is 'enryo' of Japanese students. [...] 'Enryo means thinking ahead before a situation develops, taking fully into account the other person, and then refraining from action based on the circumstance' (Yamakuse, 2011). [...T]he Japanese lose the chance to speak out on issues on the international

stage due to their tendency towards enryo. Such kinds of situations can be occurred while trying telecollaboration between Japanese students and the students in other western countries. If Japanese students [show] the attitude of 'enryo' and ask nothing, and just waiting for questions from foreign students, the foreign students can't get information from the Japanese students. Also, Japanese students can't get information from foreign students. This may not [be] beneficial for each and not very interactive. So, before carrying out lectures or class[es] with telecollaboration, we have to make students be more active enough to ask what they want to know" (Year 2 Student 1, Caluianu, 2018, p. 67).

"[A]s always, we took time and hesitated to answer questions from the Brasov side [...], partly because we had to figure out what was our opinion on matters 'as a group'. One cannot just say whatever he/she thinks as a response or opinion of the group, and this is just as Yamakuse (2011) points out in the chapter [on] 'harmony', saying that the Japanese value 'is placed on understanding those with whom one must interact and on taking action in groups" (Year 2 Student 2, Caluianu, 2018, p. 63).

"On top of that, the subject matter was cultural[ly different], so we, as a small group of [...] five members, needed to pay extra caution to decide the answer which should be able to represent the general opinion of Japanese people. We, however, would never be able to have more natural, smooth conversations if we tried to make 'agreement[s]' carefully on every single question asked by the other group, so students and teachers should be encouraged to be aware of that" (Year 2 Student 2).

These remarks are interesting because they put in a different perspective two characteristics of Japanese students that are frequently referred to critically by Western instructors: the Japanese shyness and the long silences. It is also interesting to note that, while in the case of 'enryo'/shyness, the student feels the need for coaching in order to move closer to the Western standard; in the case of 'harmony', the student does not propose to compromise and adopt the

Western standard. Instead, the student highlights the feelings of responsibility which justify the long silences and argues for a more equitable use of time. The new structure of the project offered the instructor a deeper understanding and appreciation for the students. Qualities previously taken for granted were recognized (see Burada, 2018), and apparent shortcomings appeared in a more favorable light, prompting a more student-centered organization of the collaboration.

One of the main goals of the project was to foster cultural self-awareness through exposure to a different culture. The initial curriculum was designed with the purpose of providing the widest possible range of opportunities for intercultural exchange. The exchanges were carefully planned and scheduled by the instructors, the activities were carried out smoothly and without incident. The project seemed to be very successful until comparison with the streamlined version of the second year revealed some flaws in its design. The activity-rich initial design was too product-oriented and offered too little opportunity for reflection. Although the students were presented with numerous culturally significant situations and materials, they were not given any guidelines for interpreting them. The tightly run, teacher-led schedule proceeded without incidents but also without opportunities for unscripted exchanges. It became clear that, for the project to achieve its goal, the focus of the collaboration should shift from task completion to reflection and discussion of the exchange process. The participants in the exchange should be provided with some cultural guidelines, and the 'clash of cultural fault lines' discussed in Beltz (2002) should be encouraged.

4. Conclusions

The fate of the OUC-TUB project indicates that a collaboration may fall short of its main goals even when it is carefully planned and enthusiastically carried out: the very complexity of the design may harm a project. As the project was forced to reduce its size, it became clear that excessive focus on the tasks may put the goals in jeopardy. Although cultural self-awareness seems to grow automatically once learners from different cultures come into contact, a large number of collaborative activities and a strong online presence do not guarantee deeper cross-cultural understanding if time and attention are not set aside for cross-cultural reflection.

References

Beltz, J. (2002). Social dimensions of telecollaborative foreign language study. *Language Learning & Technology, 6*(1), 60-81.

Burada, M. (2018). Argument features in novice L2 writing. A contrastive approach. *Linguaculture, 9*(1), 107-126.

Caluianu, D. (2018). Telecollaboration: foreign language education in the digital age. *Otaru University of Commerce, The review of liberal arts, 135*, 49-74.

O'Dowd, R., & Ware, P. (2009). Critical issues in telecollaborative task design. *Computer Assisted Language Learning, 22*(2), 173-188. https://doi.org/10.1080/09588220902778369

Rodas-Pérez, C., Villamediana-González, L., Chala, P. A., & Rico, C. (2018). *Virtual intercultural immersion programme: a task based learning approach and its application for assessment.* Paper presented at the 3rd UNICollaboration Conference in Krakow.

Yamakuse, Y. (2011). *Heart & soul of the Japanese.* IBC Publishing.

2. Mainstreaming virtual mobility – helping teachers to get onboard

Alastair Creelman[1] and Corina Löwe[2]

Abstract

Despite many innovative initiatives, virtual mobility is still a relatively unexploited aspect of internationalisation at European universities. An internal project at Linnaeus University, Global Classroom, aimed to create a framework and organisation to establish international networking and online collaboration as key elements of all degree programmes. The project aimed to promote the concept of virtual mobility and inspire faculty to adopt it in their degree programmes. A self-evaluation tool was developed for use in workshops, allowing faculty to highlight potential development areas. Each programme team could then implement an action plan in order to achieve these objectives, in consultation with the project team. The project also developed a toolbox for digital collaboration and worked with other institutions to offer an online collaborative course for teachers in the art of online collaboration. Another important issue was to create incentives for teachers to work with virtual mobility, including the use of digital badges. This paper describes these initiatives and discusses how virtual mobility can be mainstreamed, and what types of incentives are needed as a catalyst for development.

Keywords: mobility, internationalisation, collaboration, evaluation, project.

---

1. Linnaeus University, Kalmar, Sweden; alastair.creelman@lnu.se

2. Linnaeus University, Växjö, Sweden; corina.lowe@lnu.se

How to cite this chapter: Creelman, A., & Löwe, C. (2019). Mainstreaming virtual mobility – helping teachers to get onboard. In A. Turula, M. Kurek & T. Lewis (Eds), *Telecollaboration and virtual exchange across disciplines: in service of social inclusion and global citizenship* (pp. 15-22). Research-publishing.net. https://doi.org/10.14705/rpnet.2019.35.935

Chapter 2

1. Introduction

An internal project at Linnaeus university in Sweden, Global Classroom (2014-2017), aimed at creating a framework to make internationalisation an integrated part of all degree programmes through increased use of virtual mobility[3]. The concept of virtual mobility can be defined as

> "a form of learning which consists of virtual components through an [information and communications technology] supported learning environment that includes cross-border collaboration with people from different backgrounds and cultures working and studying together, having, as its main purpose, the enhancement of intercultural understanding and the exchange of knowledge" (Bijnens et al., 2006, p. 26).

Related to but not synonymous with virtual mobility is the more familiar concept of internationalisation at home: "the process of integrating an international, intercultural, or global dimension into the purpose, functions, or delivery of post-secondary education" (Knight, 2004, p. 11). We saw virtual mobility as the digital expression of internationalisation at home and that the two concepts complemented one another as well as complementing traditional physical mobility. The main benefit is to offer both students and faculty the opportunity to work in an international environment, even if they were unable to take part in physical mobility programmes, in line with the concept of the internationalised curriculum (Beelen & Jones, 2015). The project aimed to:

- integrate internationalisation into everyday activities,
- disseminate good practice within the university,
- strengthen awareness of inclusion and cultural diversity,
- enhance collaboration with partner universities, and
- strengthen the university's profile as a modern, international university.

---

3. https://lnu.se/en/meet-linnaeus-university/collaborate-with-us/projects-and-networks/global-classroom/

Awareness of virtual mobility was extremely low at the university when the project started, and we decided to work in three key areas: awakening **interest** in mobility using digital media, developing an **infrastructure** for virtual mobility, and developing **incentives** for staff involvement. In terms of awakening interest, we arranged regular workshops, presented the project at many departmental meetings, launched a website, and worked closely with faculty developing virtual mobility initiatives. Infrastructure development focussed on providing a toolkit for teachers with digital tools for collaborative learning, a self-assessment guide for internationalisation as well as offering guides on how to find suitable partner universities for collaboration activities. In terms of incentives, we introduced the concept of open badges as a method for rewarding students who got involved in mobility activities as well as a potential reward for teachers who organise or are involved in internationalisation activities.

2. Implementation

2.1. Internationalisation self-evaluation

The path towards virtual mobility is long and is best negotiated in small steps. It starts with informal and relatively ad hoc contacts and limited activities with teachers and students at other institutions, and can be developed up to the level of establishing online joint or double degrees with partner universities. The project wanted to encourage small-step development using a wide range of methods, platforms, and tools, and stressed that responsibility for the development lies with the teachers and their faculties.

A self-evaluation grid was developed in order to make teachers and in particular programme coordinators more aware of the level of internationalisation in their degree programmes. The grid consists of internationalisation criteria (both virtual mobility and physical mobility) on five levels from *initial* to *enhanced* and from four different perspectives: university, faculty, staff, student. In our workshops, the teachers noted all the criteria that were already met in their programmes and then identified the criteria they would like to meet within the next year or

Chapter 2

two. They could then discuss with colleagues from other programmes about how they had met their criteria and learn from each other. Then the programme team drew up an action plan on how to meet the identified criteria within a reasonable deadline. The project team could then provide support for this process, but support could also come from other departments or with the help of, for example, educational technologists or internationalisation specialists.

2.2. Toolkit for digital collaboration

For many teachers, the challenge of introducing virtual mobility into their courses lies in the pedagogical use of digital platforms and tools. The university's learning management system is designed primarily for registered students, and is not the most flexible environment for online collaboration between students or teachers from different institutions. There is a bewildering range of net-based digital platforms and tools, mostly free or at a very low cost, and this diversity is a major barrier for teachers who find it impossible to choose the right tool for their course activities.

To assist teachers in this, the project developed an online toolkit: *tools for virtual mobility*. The main feature of this was a guide to online tools for collaboration, *smarter collaboration*, with a carefully selected range of tools categorised under functions such as collaborative writing, shared workspace, curation, news gathering, screencasting, networking, e-meetings, and mind-mapping. In addition, we provided guides to finding suitable partner universities for mobility activities, how to develop potential international projects, and a guide to various forms of open education.

2.3. Teacher development

Virtual mobility can also be extended to teacher development, even in internal training courses. A good example of providing an international perspective to internal staff development is the open online course Open Networked Learning (ONL) that Linnaeus University has helped to develop in partnership with two other Swedish universities, Karolinska Institutet and Lund University (https://opennetworkedlearning.wordpress.com). The course was developed in 2014 and was largely based on an earlier model, *flexible, distance, and online learning* (Nerantzi & Gossman, 2015; Nerantzi & Uhlin, 2012), that has inspired several other spin-off courses. The course, aimed at teachers and educational technologists, offers the chance to investigate open online learning by working in small learning groups. The guiding principle of the course is learning by doing, and participants work in international online groups on collaborative problem-solving activities. In addition to the main partner universities, each course has several other partner institutions from Sweden, Finland, and South Africa. The participants from each institution receive internal recognition for completing the course, but benefit from working in mixed groups from different countries. The course is also available to a limited number of open learners, and has participants from all over the world, for example from Poland, Australia, Pakistan, and Sudan, thus raising the international profile of the course.

ONL gives first-hand experience of virtual mobility, using digital platforms and tools to solve problems in both synchronous online meetings as well as asynchronous spaces. One important factor in the success of the course is the attention given to creating a sense of community and mutual support from the very start, following the five step model of Salmon (2013). Once this community spirit is established, the problem-based learning groups work extremely tightly and the participants develop their professional networks. By letting teachers experiment with online collaboration in a course like this, we hope that they will then transfer these skills and apply them to their own courses, encouraging increased international networking and collaborative activities for their students.

2.4. Student virtual mobility

Although the project itself did not have the resources or time to directly work with student virtual mobility, there was support available to faculty who wished to do this. One example of testing virtual mobility for students was by integrating a Massive Open Online Course (MOOC) into a regular campus course in the language department for students learning how to write academic papers in

German. Foreign language teaching in the Swedish university context must meet the challenges of providing a solid education against the background of declining student numbers and thus reduced financial resources and only a few lecturers. Integrating MOOCs is one way of saving resources in the classroom. It also makes it easy for students to broaden the circle of teachers by listening to lectures with other native speakers, thus practising their listening skills. In the course module 'Academic writing', regular lectures were replaced by online lectures, and working material from the MOOC '*Wissenschaftliches Denken, Arbeiten und Schreiben*' from University of Applied Sciences, Münster, provided by the platform IVERSITY. The students worked with the MOOC material mainly at home. Seminars and the liberated lecture time was used to answer questions and for individually mentoring the writing process. The students responded positively to this method. A positive side effect was that students engaged more in taking responsibility for their learning results and worked in teams, discussing their thesis projects and peer-reviewing the work in progress. Cooperative learning activities tend "to result in higher achievement, greater long-term retention of what is learned, more frequent use of higher-level reasoning and meta-cognitive thought, more accurate and creative problem solving, more willingness to take on difficult tasks and persist in working toward goal accomplishment" (Johnson, Johnson, & Smith, 2007, p. 19). In our case, this could be verified by the teacher as well as by the good student results. The satisfaction with the pilot led to a new edition the following year.

3. Discussion – from project to mainstream

The project ended in 2017 and the question immediately arose; how do we move from project to mainstream? At the time of writing (July 2018) there is no new official virtual mobility initiative at Linnaeus University, and this raises concerns about the sustainability of initiatives like this. The project succeeded in raising awareness of virtual mobility, and has helped many teachers to start planning virtual mobility activities into their courses. We have guides, toolboxes, and self-assessment available for teachers who want to get started, and we have a network of colleagues who can assist. However, what is most needed is full top management support and the integration of virtual mobility into the university's internationalisation strategy. Furthermore there is still a degree of scepticism regarding online education among faculty and management and that, together with established traditional practice, creates considerable barriers to innovative practice.

The challenges of mainstreaming virtual mobility can be divided under three key factors: incentives, strategy, and culture.

3.1. Incentives

Teachers already have extremely busy schedules with more and more expected of them each year, often within shrinking budgets. The benefits of innovations like virtual mobility must be presented very clearly and reinforced by a range of incentives. These include recognition of initiative and innovative practice in the form of certificates (including badges), awards (internationalisation initiative of the year), career development, and financial incentives. If internationalisation is added as a mandatory element of annual appraisal interviews and competence development is available, this can support the process.

3.2. Strategy

The danger of bottoms-up grassroots projects is that they can only have limited effect if not met by top management commitment. To succeed with virtual mobility or any similar concept, it must be explicit in institutional strategy and clear overall responsibility must be assigned to a member of top management.

3.3. Culture

A culture of innovation must be clearly established where innovative practice is both encouraged and rewarded, something which is much easier said than done in today's increasingly result-oriented higher education. Teachers need time and support to be able to test new ideas such as virtual mobility. Universities need to promote teamwork as the dominant model for all course design, where teachers work in close consultation with educational technologists, librarians, and internationalisation experts.

4. Conclusion

Virtual mobility offers a more inclusive approach to internationalisation for both students and faculty, allowing opportunities for professional networking and knowledge-sharing, collaborative projects, common courses and joint/double degrees. Projects like the one described in this article can raise awareness, stimulate development, and share experience, but the real key to mainstream adoption is the integration of the concept into top management policy and full support from faculty management. Making that connection with mainstream practice is the real challenge ahead for internationalisation in higher education.

References

Beelen, J., & Jones, E. (2015). Redefining internationalization at home. *The European Higher Education Area*, 59-72. https://doi.org/10.1007/978-3-319-20877-0_5

Bijnens, H., Boussemaere, M., Rajagopal, K., Op de Beeck, I., & Van Petegem, W. (2006). *European cooperation in education through virtual mobility: a best-practice manual*. Europace.

Johnson, D., Johnson, R., & Smith, K. (2007). The state of cooperative learning in postsecondary and professional settings. *Educational Psychology Review, 19*(1), 15-29. https://doi.org/10.1007/s10648-006-9038-8

Knight, J. (2004). Internationalization remodelled: definition, approaches, and rationales. *Journal of Studies in International Education, 8*(1), 5-31. https://doi.org/10.1177/1028315303260832

Nerantzi, C., & Gossman, P. (2015). Towards collaboration as learning: evaluation of an open CPD opportunity for HE teachers. *Research in Learning Technology, 23*, 1-14. https://doi.org/10.3402/rlt.v23.26967

Nerantzi, C., & Uhlin, L. (2012). *FDOL design*. https://fdol.wordpress.com/fdol131/design/

Salmon, J. (2013). *E-tivities: the key to active online learning* (2nd ed.). Routledge.

3 From 'CoCo' to 'FloCoCo': the evolving role of virtual exchange (practice report)

Régine Barbier[1] and Elizabeth Benjamin[2]

Abstract

'CoCo' (Coventry-Colmar) is an online international learning exchange project involving students of French and International Relations at Coventry University (CU) and Networks and Telecommunications Engineering students at the Université de Haute-Alsace (UHA) in Colmar, France, running since 2014. In 2018, the exchange gained a new member through merging with an existing exchange between Coventry University and the Centro Florida Universitària (FU), in Valencia, Spain, becoming 'FloCoCo'. Where CoCo allowed for language and intercultural exchange between paired groups of UHA and CU students, FloCoCo now brings together FU, UHA and CU students, who complete a series of culture-based tasks, developing skills relating to intercultural communication and 'global citizenship' that are valued by today's graduate employers. Like its predecessor, FloCoCo aims at enhancing participants' intercultural awareness, communicative competence and digital fluency, providing an opportunity for 'virtual' international mobility and international intercultural online exchange. The following practice report discusses the most recent two iterations of FloCoCo in the context of the history of the exchange, drawing upon theories of (digital) discourse competence and online spaces to facilitate the best possible experience for participants in Virtual Exchanges (VEs).

---

1. Université de Haute-Alsace, Mulhouse, France; regine.barbier@uha.fr

2. Coventry University, Coventry, England; ac7390@coventry.ac.uk; https://orcid.org/0000-0003-0547-0768

How to cite this chapter: Barbier, R., & Benjamin, E. (2019). From 'CoCo' to 'FloCoCo': the evolving role of virtual exchange (practice report). In A. Turula, M. Kurek & T. Lewis (Eds), *Telecollaboration and virtual exchange across disciplines: in service of social inclusion and global citizenship* (pp. 23-29). Research-publishing.net. https://doi.org/10.14705/rpnet.2019.35.936

Chapter 3

Keywords: virtual exchange, intercultural communication, France, UK, technology enhanced language learning.

1. Introduction

VEs are taking the lead where physical mobility has become a challenge for socio-economic reasons, and Brexit may increase this trend. In this context, we wish to highlight the multifaceted benefits of the VE in a higher education setting, including the possibility of VEs compensating for the demise of physical mobility. This paper will analyse developments in the FloCoCo exchange, building upon existing literature (namely Orsini-Jones & Lee, 2018), while targeting the implications of digital innovations and political necessity for the evolving VE.

2. Theoretical and conceptual framework

Canale and Swain (1980) outlined a model for communicative competence, divided into four elements: linguistic, sociolinguistic, discourse, and strategic. Walker and White (2013) adapted this model to suit the demands of the digital age, digital communicative competence, giving the following elements: procedural, socio-digital, digital discourse, and strategic. These models are crucial to students involved in FloCoCo: most students at the partner institutions are working in (at least) their second language (L2), even though participants now use English as a lingua franca, and the exchange takes place entirely digitally.

Socio-digital competence and digital discourse competence are particularly applicable, because the former involves "understanding what is appropriate to use in different social contexts and knowledge domains, in terms of both technology and language" (Walker & White, 2013, p. 8), and the latter as "the ability to manage an extended task, possibly using several applications and/or types of equipment" (Walker & White, 2013, p. 9). Participants in FloCoCo must navigate the exchange by employing these skills: while there is much cultural crossover between France, Spain, and the UK, particularities can be hard to spot, and quickly escalate. This is particularly difficult to manage in a digital environment, as many linguistic and cultural subtleties are lost or easily misinterpreted (see Orsini-Jones & Lee, 2018).

VEs such as FloCoCo also hinge on digital concepts such as *affinity spaces*, i.e "physical or virtual places in which people develop relationships [...] based on shared interests" (Gee, 2005, p. 6), *connectivism*, i.e. "deriving competence from forming relationships" (Siemens, 2004, n.p), and *convergence culture* (Jenkins, 2006), in which the distinction between devices is broken down, and in the case of our students, where communication happens across multiple apps and fora. As a result, evolutions also occur concerning the role of the teacher as well as the student-teacher relationship.

These theories are all key to the continuing development of VE more broadly, but particularly relevant in the case of FloCoCo, as will be demonstrated below. As outlined by Orsini-Jones and Lee (2018, pp. 7-23), intercultural communicative competence continues to be relevant to the exchange, even in the wake of Brexit, but also in terms of the transition to a three-legged exchange, and particularly in combination with the theories outlined above.

3. Project practicalities

To complete FloCoCo, students at FU, CU and UHA are placed in small inter-institutional groups and have historically worked together throughout the project to complete three main tasks. The project is undertaken by staff members at participating universities (CU, UHA, and latterly FU); participants are students of languages at CU, of telecommunications at UHA, and of TEFL at FU. CoCo was historically a bilingual exchange; English became the lingua franca of the VE on its expansion into FloCoCo. Accordingly, the tasks were overhauled in the 2018 iteration of the exchange.

In **Task 1**, groups at each institution present themselves, their city, and university, through a three-minute video, in the language of the partner institution, and then comment on each other's productions. Students must take responsibility for delegation, distribution, and completion of work, as well as use of relevant technologies. Students are very interested in the lives of their peers, and tend to give very positive feedback.

Task 2, *Cultura*, is a series of short-response questionnaires exploring cultural attitudes, adapted from Furstenberg, Levet, English, and Maillet (2001). Students reflect on notions of 'home' culture and the other culture(s) represented in the collaboration. Students individually respond to word associations and short language tasks in their home institutions' L1. Groups then compare and contrast their responses, which tend to have some strong alignments but also some strong differences.

In **Task 3**, students discuss stereotypes and interview their partner group, ideally by synchronous means, but with the option to communicate asynchronously if they do not manage or are very shy. To structure their interviews, they first create a set of questions around cultural issues. This year, students were asked to consider a politically pertinent topic, as well as a more informal subject of their own choosing. Groups discussed Brexit, feminism and racism, as well as student life and related topics.

2018 saw the removal of the *Cultura* task for reasons to be detailed in the Discussion section. Task 3 was moved forward in the exchange and changed slightly to place more focus on the second part. A final task was devised to include a 'facilitated dialogue' around Taiye Selasi's (2014) TED Talk 'Don't ask me where I'm from, ask where I'm a local'.

4. Discussion

The challenges associated with facilitating a VE vary from year to year, so preparation is key, and commitment is capital. Technology, language, and motivation tend to be the dominant problems in carrying out FloCoCo, which has led to a need to adapt the tasks to suit both student requirements and the available tools. The move from a two-legged to a three-legged exchange has been challenging but predominantly positive.

For all we can say we live in a digital age, precious time continues to be wasted in the synchronous elements of the exchange. Skype and classroom technologies let down the VE continually. Thankfully, students and tutors alike are increasingly adept at convergence culture (Jenkins, 2006), switching between devices and applications to find communication solutions. This year, the project successfully integrated an unprecedented variety of apps and programmes, including Facebook, FaceTime, Snapchat, Whatsapp, Skype, as well as email and Moodle. These issues are complicated by language concerns, as the vast majority of students worry that they will not be able to make themselves understood, or understand their partners. Nonetheless, the use of different technologies has allowed the students to explore and personalise their affinity spaces (Gee, 2005), customising their interactions to suit comfort levels. We were pleased to note that this seems relatively intuitive to students, and it is perhaps the ability to do so that has fostered friendships that have long outlasted the official exchange duration. Student motivation continues to be an issue, even when they know they are assessed, which is very difficult to address. Group work can thus lead to conflict based in perceived workloads. Tutors have begun to tackle this through discussions on responsibility and its links to employment and 'real world' situations. Varying contributions can be difficult to monitor, and raise the question of whether motivation should be intrinsic to the student or a tutor's responsibility.

In terms of the tasks, some changes clearly needed making to adapt to student responses and productive outcomes. Task 1 has consistently worked well; students are keen to share experiences. However, Task 2 appears to have stagnated in recent years. *Cultura* questionnaires, though methodologically sound in their own right, have become less appropriate tools in the context of current student demographics and the increasingly *multi*cultural classroom. *Cultura* is in any case designed for a binary exchange. With the addition of the third member university, we felt the questionnaire was no longer suitable to FloCoCo, and intended to replace it, integrating a more creative task, which might unite the paired groups rather than dividing them. Task 3 could also be better adapted to broaden the students' competences in a global context. When it became clear that tasks were limiting rather than consolidating students' communicative competence, we took action to update them. This resulted in greater engagement from students, as well as more interactive affinity spaces throughout the exchange. The implementation of these changes was also made possible by the staff members at participating institutions having undertaken Erasmus+ training.

5. Conclusion

Through VE and FloCoCo, we can learn a lot about student needs in the digital age, where physical mobility is not always possible. These socio-political elements are unpredictable, but present many pedagogical opportunities. While Brexit has dominated discussions over the last two iterations of the exchange, it has led to some unexpectedly positive outcomes, as detailed below.

The VE highlights the evolving relationship between social contexts and knowledge domains, pushing Walker and White's (2013) 'socio-digital competence' beyond the language-learning classroom and into the realm of skills in global citizenship. The students must constantly negotiate intercultural (mis)communication. FloCoCo tests students' 'digital discourse competence', but despite increasing cross-platform competence, they are less able to manage extended tasks. We suggest promoting greater understanding of the wider project through small tasks with adapted links and flow, as well as more strongly promoting inter-institutional teamwork.

The question remains of whether VEs can, or should, replace physical mobility schemes. The latter very strongly develop classical communicative competences, but do not make the digital model redundant. The strongly digital VE conversely lacks the immersive capacity of the physical. Arguably, nothing can replace the benefits of physical mobility, but the VE will be crucial if it is the students' only exchange experience. Historically, it has been very difficult to arrange a physical component to this exchange. Students appear to be more invested in its digital form. The 2018 iteration of FloCoCo sought to maintain the immersive experience while remaining digital, by integrating a 'facilitated dialogue' into the exchange, to improve communication among all members. A new affinity space was also created within the existing VE, to support the development of three-legged conversations, offering a flexibility that represents a clear advantage over physical exchanges. A post-Brexit Europe may well witness increased communication with the use of similar tools within VEs.

References

Canale, M., & Swain, M. (1980). Theoretical bases of communicative approaches to second language teaching and testing. *Applied Linguistics, 1*, 1-47.

Furstenberg, G., Levet, S., English, K., & Maillet, K. (2001). Giving a virtual voice to the silent language of culture: the Cultura project. *Language Learning and Technology, 5*(1), 55-102.

Gee, J. P. (2005). Semiotic social spaces to affinity spaces: from the age of mythology to today's schools. In D. Barton & K. Tusting (Eds), *Beyond communities of practice*. Cambridge University Press. https://doi.org/10.1017/CBO9780511610554.012

Jenkins, H. (2006). *Convergence culture: where old and new media collide*. New York University Press.

Orsini-Jones, M., & Lee, F. (2018). *Intercultural communicative competence for global citizenship: identifying cyberpragmatic rules of engagement in telecollaboration*. Palgrave Macmillan. https://doi.org/10.1057/978-1-137-58103-7

Selasi, T. (2014). Don't ask me where I'm from, ask where I'm a local. *TEDGlobal*. https://www.ted.com/talks/taiye_selasi_don_t_ask_where_i_m_from_ask_where_i_m_a_local?language=en

Siemens, G. (2004). Connectivism: a learning theory for the digital age. *Elearnspace*. http://www.elearnspace.org/Articles/connectivism.htm

Walker, A., & White, G. (Eds). (2013). *Technology enhanced language learning: connecting theory and practice*. Oxford University Press.

4. Challenges of the transatlantic cross-disciplinary ENVOIE-UFRUG project

Juan Albá Duran[1] and Gerdientje Oggel[2]

Abstract

This paper reports upon the interdisciplinary exchange between a group of students at the University of Groningen (UG), The Netherlands, enrolled in a course on Hispanic literature and a group of students at the University of La Frontera (UFRO), Chile, enrolled in a course on journalism. The study focusses on three challenges: first, the way sociopolitical factors, i.e. a student strike, can affect an exchange; second, how to integrate learning goals from two disciplines in one Online Intercultural Exchange (OIE); and third, how to ensure reciprocity and interdependence between students. After describing how we addressed these challenges, we evaluate to what extent we have been successful at doing this. Departing from student and teacher surveys and field observations, we will show how the contextual constraints at socio-political, course, teacher, and learner level influenced the development of this OIE. Finally, we summarise the main lessons learned and in the conclusions we draw new lines for further improvement and research.

Keywords: interdisciplinary OIE, learning outcomes, teacher competences, reciprocity, interdependence.

---

1. University of Groningen, Groningen, The Netherlands; j.alba.duran@rug.nl

2. University of Groningen, Groningen, The Netherlands; g.a.oggel@rug.nl

How to cite this chapter: Albá Duran, J., & Oggel, G. (2019). Challenges of the transatlantic cross-disciplinary ENVOIE-UFRUG project. In A. Turula, M. Kurek & T. Lewis (Eds), *Telecollaboration and virtual exchange across disciplines: in service of social inclusion and global citizenship* (pp. 31-39). Research-publishing.net. https://doi.org/10.14705/rpnet.2019.35.937

1. Introduction

After having learnt from our experience with a similar interdisciplinary project[3], in the design phase of the ENVOIE-UFRUG project[4] involving first year Bachelor of Arts (BA) journalism students in Chile (introductory course on the fundamentals of social science) and second year European languages and cultures students (course on Hispanic culture and literature) in The Netherlands, we continued to develop solutions to two main challenges. First, how to make students with different learning objectives work together (Bueno-Alastuey & Kleban, 2016, p. 149) and, second, how to ensure that the activities generate interdependence between students to reach a common goal (Kittle & Hicks, 2009).

Throughout the exchange, additional challenges, such as the student strike, interfered in the process. After a brief description of the settings and pedagogical design, we report on the outcomes of the OIE and discuss to what extent we managed to overcome the mentioned issues. Lastly, we will establish points for improvement and draw some conclusions for future OIEs.

2. Project description

The exchange took eight weeks (April 16th to June 8th 2018). Thirteen student groups (at least two from each university) carried out three activities to collaboratively write an article for a joint intercultural magazine. For each activity they had to have at least one online meeting on a videoconferencing tool of their choice. The first activity was an icebreaker to get to know each other and write a team profile together in Padlet. The second served to write a proposal

---

3. The RUG-UB interdisciplinary telecollaboration project (2013-2017) was set up for second year students of Spanish from the department of the BA of European languages and cultures at the University of Groningen (RUG), and students from the Master of teaching Spanish as a second language from the University of Barcelona (UB); http://uni-collaboration.eu/node/1026.

4. The UFRUG project (Temuco - Groningen) is part of the umbrella project ENVOIE, funded by the University of Groningen, which has developed several OIEs between the RUG and other universities around the world and across disciplines; https://www.rug.nl/let/organization/diensten-en-voorzieningen/ictol/projecten/envoie/?lang=en.

and give peer feedback, and the third to collaboratively write the article using Google Docs (see Figure 1 for the project outline).

Figure 1. UFRUG project outline

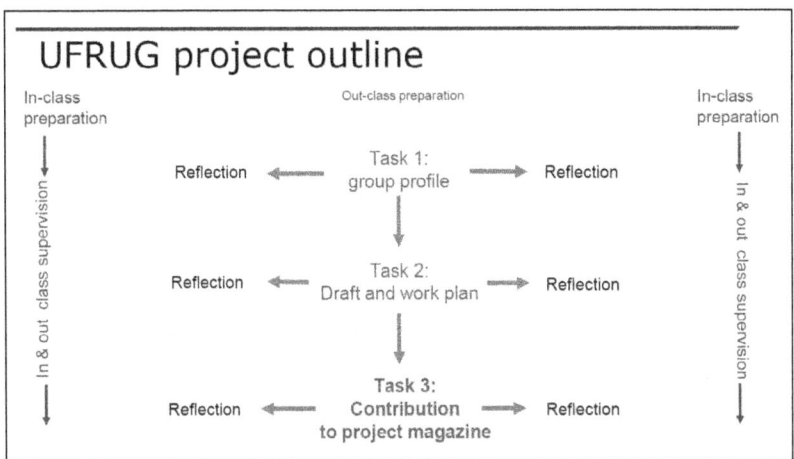

The task instructions included the learning goals of the project, which were linked to those of the courses. Students had to negotiate the topic of the article with their transatlantic partners synthesising disciplines.

Regarding reciprocity, we tried to ensure personal involvement, equal participation, and interdependence in the activities by using different dynamics: in the icebreaker by having them search for common interests, and in the next activities by prompting negotiation of content and form. In the feedback phase, students had to use their partners' comments to improve their article proposal. Additionally, the Chilean students had to provide linguistic feedback to students of Spanish as L2.

These requirements were mentioned in the instructions and assessed through questions about teamwork, team dynamics, and task content through a self-evaluation questionnaire that students completed in a Google Form after each activity.

Within the framework of ENVOIE, several team members made this project possible. Additionally to the teachers of the courses participating in the exchange, two experienced teachers in OIE (the authors of this article) had the role of task co-developers and pedagogic advisors. The tasks, group dynamics, and the final product of the OIE were agreed upon all together, but the co-developers/advisors designed most materials. The project manager and his team submitted evaluation surveys to participants at the end of the project.

3. Results

Besides the everyday communication with teachers and students and general observations, the final survey served as the main data source for a systematic analysis of the exchange (see Table 1 and Table 2), including a five point Likert scale and optional open questions. As a complementary source, the three self assessments were taken into account to see how students did or did not work together. In the magazine articles, interdisciplinarity and reciprocity were considered, i.e. (lack of) integration of topics from both disciplines and cultures, and (lack of) cohesion and coherence between parts. The data analysis shows how the development/implementation of this OIE was influenced by the challenges at socio-political, course, teacher, and learner levels.

3.1. Challenge 1: student strike

Between May 13th and July 5th there was a student strike at UFRO that paralysed all lectures and overlapped with half of the OIE. Nonetheless, the Chilean group continued participating and the UFRO teachers organised supervision meetings with them. In the survey, some UG students mention the strike as a possible reason for difficulties of communication between the groups.

3.2. Challenge 2: interdisciplinarity

As stated above, one of the main challenges was to make sure that students from the different disciplines would equally benefit from the project in terms of course related content and learning outcomes. As shown in Table 1, UG students disagree with the statements that the OIE contributed to a better understanding of the course content and that it was well integrated in the course. UFRO students are neutral about the first statement but agree with the other two.

The content of the articles in the magazine, such as *La música como elemento transcultural en los Países Bajos y Chile* and *Contrastes de la cultura gastronómica de Chile y Holanda*, shows that students did make an effort to synthesise different cultural perspectives but did not elaborate on academic, course related content.

Table 1. Ratings for Question (Q) 14: respondents' rate UG: 62.5% (20 out of 32); respondents' rate UFRO: 51.6% (16 out of 31)

	Q14.1 The OIE contributed to a better understanding of the course		Q14.9 The OIE was well-integrated in the course		Q14.8 The learning goals of the OIE for this course were clear	
	UG (%)	UFRO (%)	UG (%)	UFRO (%)	UG (%)	UFRO (%)
Completely disagree	45	6.25	35	0	20	0
Somewhat disagree	15	18.75	10	6.25	5	25
Neutral	15	50	25	12.50	35	6.25
Somewhat agree	20	25	25	37.50	20	37.50
Completely agree	5	0	5	43.75	20	31.25

3.3. Challenge 3: reciprocity and autonomy

Another challenge of the interdisciplinary character of this OIE was to design the activities in such a way that students would need the other group's expertise and collaboration to fulfill the task together. As shown in Table 2, the OIE contributed to students' ability to collaborate online and to learn autonomously. However, contrasting these results with students' reflection reports, we see that out of 13 groups, only two report having managed to collaborate without having problems of reciprocity. Except for two UFRO students, all problems were claimed by UG students saying that UFRO peers did not contribute enough. In fact, many groups did not meet the deadlines set but teachers did not always monitor this. Furthermore, the lack of coherence and differences in style and language of the articles, show that students worked mostly individually instead of collaboratively.

Table 2. Ratings from general survey Question (Q)14

	Q14.4 The OIE contributed to my ability to collaborate with others online		Q14.3 The OIE provided an environment for active learning (you were in charge of your learning and negotiated actions with your partner)	
	UG (%)	UFRO (%)	UG (%)	UFRO (%)
Completely disagree	5	25	10	0
Somewhat disagree	25	0	10	6.25
Neutral	20	6.25	15	6.25
Somewhat agree	35	37.50	30	37.50
Completely agree	15	50	35	50

Despite the careful design of the activities, the almost overall negative evaluation by UG students show that (1) the OIE did not substantially contribute to students achieving the learning objectives of their respective courses, and (2) the students did not participate equally in the activities.

The generally more positive evaluation by UFRO (teachers and students) may indicate that they were not fully aware of the complexity of the OIE and the many different aspects of it that required their attention. UFRO students might have been less critical for being first years.

4. Discussion and lessons learned

In this section we will discuss the challenges faced and give suggestions on how to deal with them in a future edition of this project.

4.1. Challenge 1: strike

According to the Chilean teachers, student strikes at the UFRO usually take place in the spring semester. For this reason and provided that courses and academic calendars match, it is recommended to schedule a next edition in the autumn semester.

4.2. Challenge 2: interdisciplinarity

An introductory course of journalism dealing with general concepts of social sciences and an advanced course on literature seem to have lacked sufficient points in common. For a next edition, we should make sure to find courses that have more synergies in terms of subject matter and learning outcomes. At the same time we should align the learning outcomes and tasks of the OIE (enhancement of intercultural and transversal skills) better with the learning outcomes of the courses.

4.3. Challenge 3: reciprocity and autonomy

The differences in learner autonomy between first and second year students might have negatively influenced the collaboration. On top of this, the Chilean teachers of the course did not receive the proper training to be prepared to give the students the guidance they needed. The fact that it was mostly the task co-designers and pedagogical advisors who created and implemented the tasks, made the teachers feel a little detached from the project. For the teachers at UFRO, this was even more the case due to the strike and also because they could not count on the support of the UG based advisors for the in-class activities (Belz, 2001). As a consequence, there was a lack of teacher monitoring of students during the implementation phase of the OIE (Melchor-Couto & Jauregi, 2016). The complexity of the tasks also might have required a too high level of student autonomy and OIE-related teacher competences. Therefore, for a next edition, it is recommended to first carry out a thorough needs analysis at both student and teacher levels before planning and developing the OIE. Full training and support should be offered to the teachers responsible for the courses and they should be the ones who design and implement the project. Finally, students should be made aware of each other's needs and learning goals to be achieved so that they can also help each other in the learning process.

5. Conclusion

This paper shows that for this interdisciplinary OIE to be successful in a next edition, special attention needs to be given to a number of intertwined challenges at socio-political, institutional, course, teacher, and learner levels. Virtual exchange teacher trainings like the ones offered through EVE[5] and EVOLVE[6] seem to be crucial. If teachers lack competences to properly guide students, student performances will automatically diminish.

The challenges which are inherent to the interdisciplinary character of the exchange need further research to be solved: Is it possible to link any course to any other one? How do we make sure each group achieves the courses' and OIEs learning outcomes? For these (and other) questions to be answered we believe the principles of reciprocity and autonomy as defined by Little and Brammerts (1996) for language tandems, need to be reframed not only at student level but also at institutional and teacher level, taking into account all the factors involved.

Acknowledgements

We thank Dr Sake Jager for his unconditional support as project manager and colleague. Our deepest gratitude also goes to all the teachers and students who made this OIE possible.

---

[5]. Erasmus+ Virtual Exchange (EVE) training programmes: https://europa.eu/youth/erasmusvirtual/activities_en

[6]. Evidence-Validated Online Learning through Virtual Exchange (EVOLVE) training programme: https://evolve-erasmus.eu/training/

References

Belz, J. A. (2001). Institutional and individual dimensions of transatlantic group work in network-based language teaching. *ReCALL, 13*(2), 129-147. https://doi.org/10.1017/S0958344001000726a

Bueno-Alastuey, M. C., & Kleban, M. (2016). Matching linguistic and pedagogical objectives in a telecollaboration project: a case study. *Computer Assisted Language Learning, 29*(1), 148-166. https://doi.org/10.1080/09588221.2014.904360

Kittle, P., & Hicks, T. (2009). Transforming the group paper with collaborative online writing. *Pedagogy: Critical Approaches to Teaching Literature, Language, Composition, and Culture, 9*(3), 525-538. https://doi.org/10.1215/15314200-2009-012

Little, D., & Brammerts, H. (Eds). (1996). A guide to language learning in tandem via the Internet. *CLCS Occasional Paper no. 46*. Trinity College, Centre for Language and Communication Studies.

Melchor-Couto, S., & Jauregi, K. (2016). Teacher competences for telecollaboration: the role of coaching. In S. Jager, M. Kurek & B. O'Rourke (Eds), *New directions in telecollaborative research and practice: selected papers from the second conference on telecollaboration in higher education* (pp. 185-192). Research-publishing.net. https://doi.org/10.14705/rpnet.2016.telecollab2016.506

5. Virtual School Garden Exchange – thinking globally, gardening locally

Johanna Lochner[1]

Abstract

This paper gives an overview of nine different Virtual School Garden Exchange (VSGE) projects. In VSGEs, learners from primary or secondary schools with school gardens exchange virtually on their garden experiences and related topics, using digital media like emails, photos, films, or videoconferences. In this manner, the global perspective of Education for Sustainable Development (ESD) can be integrated in the school garden. ESD aims to enable children, young people, and adults to think and act in a sustainable manner. It puts people in a position to make decisions for the future and to estimate how their actions affect future generations or life elsewhere in the world. In this paper, the research procedures and main results of the preliminary study of my PhD research project are presented.

Keywords: virtual exchange, school garden, education for sustainable development, global perspective.

1. Introduction

Virtual Exchange (VE) refers to "education programmes or activities in which constructive communication and interaction take place between individuals or groups who are geographically separated and/or from different cultural backgrounds, with the support of educators or facilitators" (Evolve, 2018,

---

1. Humboldt Universität zu Berlin, Berlin, Germany; lochnejo@hu-berlin.de

How to cite this chapter: Lochner, J. (2019). Virtual School Garden Exchange – thinking globally, gardening locally. In A. Turula, M. Kurek & T. Lewis (Eds), *Telecollaboration and virtual exchange across disciplines: in service of social inclusion and global citizenship* (pp. 41-47). Research-publishing.net. https://doi.org/10.14705/rpnet.2019.35.938

para. 1). An emerging form of VE for educational purposes is VSGE; it is a form of virtual international networking of learners from primary and secondary schools about their school gardens and related issues using digital media such as emails, videos, photos, or videoconferences. VSGE is an educational tool that links local gardening with global thinking. It is an attempt to integrate and implement the global perspective of ESD in local school gardens. ESD aims to enable children, young people and adults to think and act in a sustainable manner. It puts people in a position to make decisions for the future and to estimate to which extent their actions may affect future generations or life elsewhere in the world.

Since the Conference on Environment and Development of the UN in 1992 in Brazil, ESD is on the international agenda. The adopted agreement Agenda 21 captures that education has to make a significant contribution towards sustainable development (UNCED, 1992, p. 329 ff.). Since 1992, remarkable developments have occurred, e.g. in 2015, the 2030 Agenda was adopted by the UN, including the 17 Sustainable Development Goals (SDGs), and ESD as part of SDG 4 (UN, 2015). The target 4.7 of the SDG 4 'quality education' states that, by 2030, "all learners acquire the knowledge and skills needed to promote sustainable development, including, among others, through [ESD] and sustainable lifestyles, human rights, gender equality, promotion of a culture of peace and nonviolence, global citizenship and appreciation of cultural diversity and of culture's contribution to sustainable development" (UN, 2015, p. 21).

There are many different learning settings where ESD can be put into practice, school gardens are one of them. School gardens exist all around the world. They are often part of school campuses or located in close proximity and have different shapes, sizes, and purposes, e.g. learning, recreation, or food production (FAO, 2010, p. 2; Milicevic & Nowikow, 2017, p. 2). School gardens provide multiple links to global issues which can be explored: for example the different origins of the crops being cultivated in the garden, the climate that affects the gardening, or different cultural eating habits. In VSGEs learners can discuss with their peers from abroad about such topics. In this paper, the research procedures and main results of Lochner (2016) will be presented. Approaches and experiences in the implementation of VSGE as a method of ESD in school gardens will be surveyed.

2. Methodology

In this study nine VSGE projects have been identified through snowball sampling (Schnell, Hill, & Esser, 2013). Their approaches, including similarities and differences, were highlighted through standardized questionnaires and expert interviews. The experts were the coordinators of the projects.

During the analysis, the focus was on the similarities, representative statements, joint shared knowledge, relevance structures, constructions of realities, interpretations, and patterns of importance (Meuser & Nagel, 1991, p. 452). The expert interviews were analyzed in MAXQDA after the principle of qualitative content analysis by Mayring (2000).

3. Findings

The earliest developments in the practice of VSGE that I am aware of date to 2001: the 'Food for Thought School Linking Programme', a British-Ugandan joint project organized by Devon Development Education (DDE, n.d.) and the 'North-South Education School Garden' project in Germany and Ecuador from the organization Inka e. V., with a particular focus on old crop varieties (INKA e.V., 2003). Both projects mainly exchange(d) via letters, drawings, and photos. In 2004/2005 an 'International School Garden Network' between schools in Brazil, Germany, Russia, South Africa, Taiwan, and Czech Republic existed, which promoted the exchange of German school gardens with school gardens worldwide. The exchanges mainly took place between multipliers who worked with school gardens and introduced the global perspective with photos and emails into the classroom (Lochner, 2016, p. 30 ff.). A follow up project was conducted in 2013-2017 in the 'Global Classroom' project (Grüne Liga, 2018).

In 2015, three more exchanges between individual teachers from Europe and Africa and their schools during one and four months took place (Lochner, 2016, p. 33 ff.).

Two more expansive programs are the 'Global Garden Exchange E-Pen Pal Program' (GGE) from Slow Food USA and the 'Go! Global Garden' project (GGG) from the ESD Expert Net. The GGE connected 80 schools in 2016 and 2017, but end of 2017 the program was closed. GGG conducted in 2015 and 2016 two pilots with learners from South Africa, Mexico, Germany, and India exchanging via videos, photo collages, and videoconferences. GGG is now embedded in Go! Global, which is focusing more generally on VE between sustainability activities (school gardening, waste management, etc.) in schools (ESD Expert Net, n.d.).

In the years 2000-2017 the media used in the exchanges did not vary much (see Figure 1). All projects used photos, some letters and drawings, and just in two of the exchanges videos and video conferences were used (see Figure 1). The duration of the different VSGEs ranged between one and 48 months, some had just two interactions, others up to ten. Themes like varieties of plants, cultivation methods, food, cultures, climate conditions, and school life were covered.

The connecting link between the learners is the school garden. An interviewee mentions "gardens can [...] be so fundamentally unifying across cultures" (Lochner, 2016, p. 38). The conditions and actors in and with which the VSGE is implemented, like the schools, teachers, and learners, are very diverse. The experts emphasize that the peculiarity of VSGEs is the thematic focus: the common goal of growing something. An expert sees it as "good conditions to reduce prejudices and stereotypes" (Lochner, 2016, p. 39). The learners are exposed to different countries and cultures, which can encourage reflection, convey a sense of cosmopolitanism, and create space to discuss global challenges. Some experts hope that the exchange may create a sense of connectedness. Four of the experts emphasize that they want to achieve knowledge transfer, which can be knowledge regarding other cultures or garden related.

Figure 1. Different aspects of nine VSGE projects

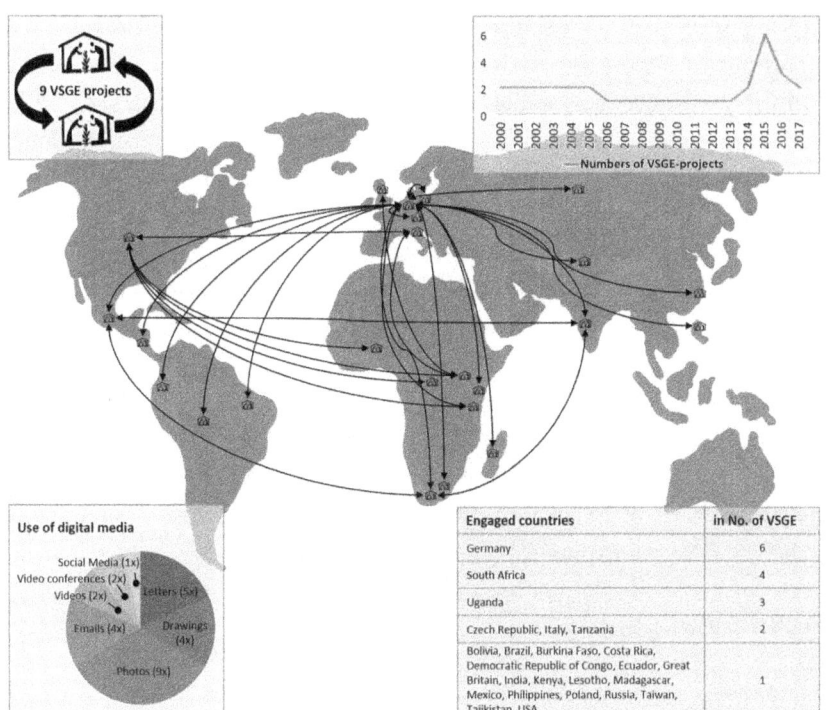

4. Conclusion

These nine VSGE projects give a first idea on how diverse but also similar such VSGEs can look like. Nine projects during nearly 20 years is not a lot, which implies that there is still limited experience with VSGE. There might exist more projects, but so far I have not been able to identify them. This can be caused by language barriers and/or the lack of a unifying terminology. Even in the identified projects the terminology was very diverse: some projects use the terms 'school linking' or 'twinning'. One project calls it 'international school garden networking'.

In literature, VSGE seems to be nearly non existent. To prove this, in the next step of my research I reviewed 158 peer-reviewed articles related to school gardening to identify research on VSGE or similar approaches (Lochner, Rieckmann, & Robischon, forthcoming). To find out how participation in a VSGE affects learners, I will conduct qualitative expert interviews with teachers who have been engaged in VSGEs and can be seen as experts for their learners' learning processes. Furthermore I will conduct group interviews with participating learners at the end of the exchange.

My research focuses on school gardens in primary and secondary schools, but of course VE can be also implemented between other types of gardens. Why not linking two university gardens?

This paper and future research shall help to establish the terminology of VSGE, to be able to identify projects, to share experiences, and to contribute to a more frequent practice of VSGE.

Acknowledgements

I want to acknowledge my two supervisors Prof. Marcel Robischon and Prof. Marco Rieckmann and Dr Detlef Virchow, my master thesis supervisor, for their support and constructive feedback and the Heinrich Böll Foundation for my PhD scholarship.

References

DDE. (n. d.). *Food for thought: school gardens link-up.* http://www.globalcentredevon.org.uk/images/stories/FFT-School_Gardens_Link-Up_leaflet_final_for_email.pdf

ESD Expert Net. (n. d.). „Go! Global" - Virtueller Schulaustausch. https://esd-expert.net/go-global-virtueller-schulaustausch.html

Evolve. (2018). *What is virtual exchange?* https://evolve-erasmus.eu/about-evolve/what-is-virtual-exchange/

FAO. (2010). *A new deal for school gardens*. Rome.

Grüne Liga. (2018). *Global classroom: students-projects for sustainable life*. Gardening. http://globalclassroom.de/category/gardening/

INKA e.V. (2003). *Bildung Nord-Süd: Schulgärten - Kulturpflanzenvielfalt*. http://www.inka-ev.de/deutsch/schulprojekt.htm

Lochner, J. (2016). *Globales Lernen in lokalen Schulgärten durch virtuellen Schulgartenaustausch: Erfahrungen, Herausforderungen und Lösungsansätze (Master of Public Policy)*. Europa-Universität Viadrina, Frankfurt Oder. https://www.wusgermany.de/sites/wusgermany.de/files/content/files/lochner2_0.pdf

Lochner, J., Rieckmann, M., & Robischon, M. (forthcoming). *Any sign of virtual school garden exchanges? Education for sustainable development in school gardens since 1992*.

Mayring, P. (2000). Qualitative content analysis. *Forum Qualitative Sozialforschung / Forum: Qualitative Social Research, 1*(2). https://doi.org/10.17169/FQS-1.2.1089

Meuser, M., & Nagel, U. (1991). ExpertInneninterviews - vielfach erprobt, wenig bedacht: ein Beitrag zur qualitativen Methodendiskussion. In D. Garz & K. Kraimer (Eds), *Qualitativ-empirische Sozialforschung* (pp. 441-468). Westdeutscher-Verlag. https://doi.org/10.1007/978-3-322-97024-4_14

Milicevic, M., & Nowikow, U. (Eds). (2017). *School garden root network*. Berlin. https://www.grueneliga-berlin.de/wp-content/uploads/2017/08/School-Garden-Root-Network-Magazin.pdf

Schnell, R., Hill, P. B., & Esser, E. (2013). *Methoden der empirischen Sozialforschung* (10th ed.). Oldenbourg.

UN. (2015). *Transforming our world: the 2030 agenda for sustainable development*. http://www.un.org/ga/search/view_doc.asp?symbol=A/RES/70/1&Lang=E

UNCED. (1992). *Agenda 21*. http://www.un.org/depts/german/conf/agenda21/agenda_21.pdf

6 'FORE - UEK Telecollaboration 2017' – virtual exchange in business studies

Małgorzata Marchewka[1] and Reeta Raina[2]

Abstract

The report describes the FORE - UEK Telecollaboration 2017 project conducted between November 25th 2017 and January 3rd 2018 between over 60 students from FORE School of Management, India (hereafter FORE), and 70 students from Cracow University of Economics, Poland, and Erasmus students (hereafter UEK). The main goal of the project was to enhance the understanding of managerial problems in modern business. Apart from learning outcomes in the area of management and business communication, the aim of the project was to create learning environment facilitating the understanding of the problems of cross-cultural communication, as well as development of attitudes of cooperation and sensitivity to cultural differences. The report contains detailed information about organizational matters related to the project, such as: initial arrangements, choice of tasks, scheduling, tools, description of participants, learning outcomes, and evaluation of the project from the perspective of teachers and students and the conclusions for further cooperation.

Keywords: telecollaboration, business studies, cross-cultural communication.

---

1. Cracow University of Economics, Cracow, Poland; marchewm@uek.krakow.pl

2. FORE School of Management, New Delhi, India; rraina@fsm.ac.in

How to cite this chapter: Marchewka, M., & Raina, R. (2019). 'FORE - UEK Telecollaboration 2017' – virtual exchange in business studies. In A. Turula, M. Kurek & T. Lewis (Eds), *Telecollaboration and virtual exchange across disciplines: in service of social inclusion and global citizenship* (pp. 49-55). Research-publishing.net. https://doi.org/10.14705/rpnet.2019.35.939

Chapter 6

1. Introduction

Telecollaboration is an engagement of students in online cross-cultural interactions with foreign partners in order to gain mutual educational benefits. The method is broadly used in language learning, but in recent years the idea has evolved in different areas of education as well (O'Dowd, 2018). Virtual exchange is a unique opportunity to let students from different countries and cultures to work together on common problems, which in case of a presented project are business and management. The value of telecollaboration is particularly visible in cooperation between students coming from very distant countries, such as India and Poland, when online collaboration is the simplest way to create a safe environment in which participants can experience cultural differences and can try to cope with them themselves. It requires cross-cultural communication, managing cross-cultural teams, and, in the field of business studies, multidimensional reflection on managerial issues.

2. Project organization

2.1. Objectives

The main goal of the FORE - UEK Telecollaboration 2017 project was to enhance the understanding of managerial problems in modern international business and to develop attitudes of cooperation and sensitivity to cultural differences. Moreover, for Polish students, the goal was to practice English. In general, similarly to other projects, our long-term goal was to prepare students to work in multinational communities (Abruquah, Dosa, & Duda, 2016).

2.2. Participants

The participants were both undergraduates and postgraduates. In the case of the Polish students, their language levels ranged from A1 to C1. Seventy students of UEK and 64 students of FORE were divided into 24 multicultural teams of five to seven members.

For some students, the participation was mandatory (as a part of the course activity), for some others it was a voluntary project for which they could gain additional points for their final grades.

2.3. Tasks

Task design is important as it initiates cooperation, marks the presence of teachers, and determines group processes (Kurek, 2015). Our telecollaboration was divided into two parts: team building, and a team project on a chosen managerial topic. In the first part, teams were asked to design a team flower illustrating similarities between members (middle part of a flower) and including specific information about each team member in a separate patel (Figure 1).

Figure 1. Example of a team flower (Source: FORE-UEK Telecollaboration 2017, students' work)

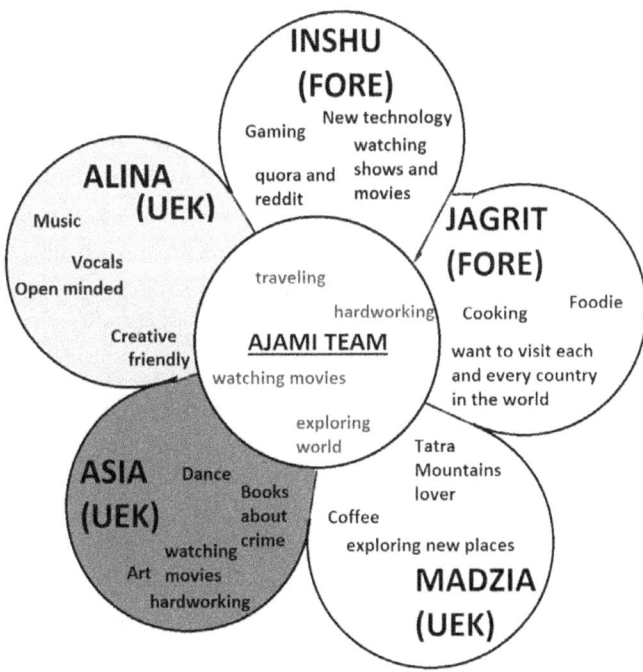

Chapter 6

During the second part of the telecollaboration, students were asked to discuss and present a poster regarding one of the following topics:

- Global business – a challenge for modern managers. Indian and Polish perspective.

- How to make business in Poland and in India.

- How to be a good manager. Indian and Polish perspective.

- Conflict management – ways of reacting to disagreement. The case of Poland and India.

- 'Getting lost in translation' – different communication styles. The case of India and Poland

- Similarities and differences between Polish and Indian tradition.

According to original arrangements, the telecollaboration was supposed to begin on November 25th 2017 and last three weeks: the first part was planned for one week, and the second for two weeks. However, because of an initial delay (due to huge interest among FORE students, official approval by FORE Programme Board was required), exam sessions at FORE, Christmas being celebrated at UEK, and New Year celebrations, the deadline for final submission of the projects was prolonged, and in total the cooperation lasted for seven weeks.

2.4. Tools

The main tool used in the telecollaboration was the Padlet.com platform. It served as a communication tool between teachers and students and it was used for the presentation of team results. Assuming that even the simplest tools, such as email, are enough to design learning activities enabling cooperation between students from different locations (Harris, 1999), students were free to choose tools for their team work at their convenience. According to the survey conducted after the project, 65% of the respondents declared that their team organized a teleconference for all team members, and over 80% of respondents admitted that their team created a group in one of the communicators (e.g. Facebook Messenger, WhatsApp).

3. Results

In the case of virtual exchange in business studies, two types of results are expected: one related to deepening understanding of managerial problems, and another to the development of communication skills.

Interculturality of the exchange determines a dual approach to managerial issues, based on different values and assumptions embedded in the culture. Students learned how the same problem, such as team leading, entrepreneurship, and global management, may be approached in two different cultures. Such a reflection broadens the understanding of these issues.

Additionally, virtual exchange is also a source of reflection on communication patterns and cross-cultural differences in communication. Given that the role of teachers was limited and teams were self-organizing, it was an opportunity to manage an international team. Eventually, 22 teams managed to accomplish both tasks.

Students' evaluations of the project were positive. Below, some of their opinions on benefits and challenges are presented:

> "The most inspiring was collaborating over such long distance and breaking barriers".

> "Thanks to this cooperation, we could meet a new culture, broaden our horizons, and most importantly, gain new great friends. Our chat was not limited only to the task. We sent pictures from our countries and from our universities. We wanted to learn about ourselves as much as possible".

Chapter 6

> "The most challenging was to connect in the same time. Everyone have own responsibilities, and it was not always possible to contact at the same time".
>
> "The most difficult step was the first step. As soon as we started the group chat, a thread of understanding was established between us".

The general observation is that students were more focused on cross-cultural communication than on business issues. Whereas for some students the telecollaboration project was great fun and they kept exchanging pictures and news after it had been finished, for others it was a source of great frustration, as they faced problems with organizing team work. The most common constraints were: time difference, time perception and other cultural differences, age difference, and unequal contribution to the group work.

4. Conclusions

Nowadays, when business and management students must be ready to work in international environments, virtual exchange is a wonderful experience enabling students to identify their strengths and areas of competences that should be improved. Telecollaboration in business studies not only facilitates the discussion on particular managerial problems, but also helps to develop skills such as team management, team communication, presentation, and team problem solving.

The main achieved outcome is deeper understanding of cross-cultural communication. Moreover, according to the results of the survey, the majority of respondents were very glad with their team work results and new experience. Overall evaluation of the project and the benefits for students and teachers lead to a conclusion that the project was worth the effort.

As for the organization of virtual exchange, future projects should last longer than the initially planned three weeks. Especially the first phase of team building must be extended. Moreover, given that some teams had problems with self-organization, the activities should be more structured (e.g. plan of the first meeting, tools).

Our project also brings insights into the role of a teacher in telecollaboration. Even though we decided to limit our interventions, we kept modeling behaviors by posting our opinions, commenting students' work, and taking part in the discussion. However, according to our observations, some students require more interference from a teacher.

References

Abruquah, E., Dosa, I., & Duda, G. (2016). Telecollaboration, challenges and opportunities. In S. Jager, M. Kurek & B. O'Rourke (Eds), *New directions in telecollaborative research and practice: selected papers from the second conference on telecollaboration in higher education* (pp. 105-111). Research-publishing.net. https://doi.org/10.14705/rpnet.2016.telecollab2016.496

Harris, J. (1999). First steps in telecollaboration. *Learning & Leading with Technology, 27*(3), 54-57. http://virtual-architecture.wm.edu/Foundation/Articles/First-Steps.pdf

Kurek, M. (2015). Designing tasks for complex virtual learning environments. *Bellaterra Journal of Teaching & Learning Language & Literature, 8*(2), 13-32. https://doi.org/10.5565/rev/jtl3.633

O'Dowd, R. (2018). From telecollaboration to virtual exchange: state-of-the-art and the role of UNICollaboration in moving forward. *Journal of Virtual Exchange, 1*, 1-23. Research-publishing.net. https://doi.org/10.14705/rpnet.2018.jve.1

7. When two worldviews meet: promoting mutual understanding between 'secular' and religious students of Islamic studies in Russia and the United States

Alexander Knysh[1], Anna Matochkina[2], Daria Ulanova[3], Philomena Meechan[4], and Todd Austin[5]

Abstract

The authors discuss results from two co-taught courses in Islamic studies shared as a virtual exchange between the University of Michigan (U-M), USA, and Saint Petersburg State University (SPbU), Russia. These courses were shared with the intent of expanding the range of perspectives to which the students were exposed and to provide an opportunity to experience the approach to education and to the subject studied in the partner country. The SPbU student cohort included graduates of Islamic religious colleges from across Russia who studied along with non-religious students specializing in Islamic studies. The U-M cohort included students of diverse religious, ethnic, and national backgrounds. International teams met outside class to prepare questions for the weekly synchronous whole-class discussions and to create a final group presentation.

---

1. University of Michigan, Ann Arbor, Michigan, United States and Saint Petersburg State University, Saint Petersburg, Russia; alknysh@umich.edu; https://orcid.org/0000-0002-2791-8976

2. Saint Petersburg State University, Saint Petersburg, Russia; anna-matochkina@yandex.ru

3. Saint Petersburg State University, Saint Petersburg, Russia; d.ulanova@spbu.ru

4. University of Michigan, Ann Arbor, Michigan, United States; phili@umich.edu

5. University of Michigan, Ann Arbor, Michigan, United States; laustin@umich.edu; https://orcid.org/0000-0003-0717-3759

How to cite this chapter: Knysh, A., Matochkina, A., Ulanova, D., Meechan, P., & Austin, T. (2019). When two worldviews meet: promoting mutual understanding between 'secular' and religious students of Islamic studies in Russia and the United States. In A. Turula, M. Kurek & T. Lewis (Eds), *Telecollaboration and virtual exchange across disciplines: in service of social inclusion and global citizenship* (pp. 57-64). Research-publishing.net. https://doi.org/10.14705/rpnet.2019.35.940

Chapter 7

Keywords: virtual exchange, telecollaboration, online intercultural exchange, religious studies, Islamic studies.

1. Introduction

Our international team of instructors and instructional technologists hereby presents results from two courses in Islamic studies shared between the U-M and SPbU. In winter 2017, we team-taught the course 'Islamic Intellectual History', and in fall 2017, 'Islamic Mysticism: Sufism in Space and Time'. Our joint venture was inspired in part by the efforts of the governments of the Russian Federation and the European Union to integrate Muslims into mainstream culture and society.

In Russia, in 2013, the Council of the Muftis of the Russian Federation headed by the chief religious authority, Mufti Ravil Gaynetdin, and his associates came together with a few forward-looking leaders of religious and 'secular' (i.e. with no declared religious affiliation) institutions of higher learning to launch an experiment in 'integrated education'. This effort brought together graduates of Islamic religious colleges (*madrasas*) with SPbU students to pursue Bachelor of Arts (BA) and Master of Arts (MA) degrees in Islamic studies as an academic, rather than as a religious subject.

The U-M cohort consisted of students of diverse religious, ethnic, and national backgrounds, including practicing and non-practicing Muslims from the Middle East, Africa, and South Asia.

In the world of virtual exchange, shared courses on the study of religion remain a rarity. In their 2019 chapter, Dorroll, Hall, and Baumi (2019) describe virtual ethnography collaborations between Christian students in the United States and Muslim students in Egypt to foster cross-cultural and cross-religious engagement.

2. Course description

The courses were structured around the 'shared syllabus' model described by O'Dowd (2018). The 12 students at each university interacted both in 24-person all-group weekly meetings and in small three or four person groups outside of class.

The full class was connected for live discussions using formal videoconferencing systems. To facilitate the sharing of documents and occasional recording, connections were made through the BlueJeans cloud service. Discussions were conducted in English with occasional recourse to Russian and Arabic. Translation was provided by both instructors and students. The classes were assigned the same readings on the weeks' subjects. Texts were mostly in English with occasional use of Russian translations, if available, as an option.

The small cross-institutional groups met outside of class, with their composition determined by the students' level of study (bachelors, masters, or doctoral), shared academic interests, and language skills. Following the telecollaborative task categories outlined in O'Dowd and Ware (2009), the teams discussed the readings and formulated weekly discussion questions that constituted the foundation of joint class sessions. Additionally, each small group created a presentation on a mutually-agreed topic based upon their personal and academic interests. These were presented at the end of the semester in joint sessions. For communication, students chose the tools that best fitted their needs, including email, WhatsApp, Facebook, Skype, and Google tools.

At the completion of the courses, feedback was collected from the students at both universities through the use of written surveys and personal interviews. The surveys were offered in both Russian and English through the Qualtrics platform, with an eye toward consistency across courses and the accumulation of comparable data. Personal interviews were conducted face-to-face or on the BlueJeans platform.

3. Discussion

Both the all-group weekly meetings and the small-group interactions outside of class led to enriching perspective-taking experiences for the students. This was true both with regard to their study of the subject material and to their exposure to the differing cultures, religious denominations, and educational systems.

Within the small groups, advanced students significantly enriched the academic expertise of their partners, stimulating them to consider more deeply one or another aspect of the topic. As an example, one student altered the subject of her graduate thesis in response to conversations she held with her group partner. Students also reported pushing boundaries, working with resources that were not represented in their curriculum or not available to others in their group. For example, one group chose to present on the difference between the Ash'arites and the Maturidi theological doctrine, the latter being routinely neglected in American survey courses on Islam in favor of the former.

In the classroom, there was a marked difference between religious and 'secular' students in the way they argued and defended their respective positions. Answering questions or advocating their viewpoints, religious students presented arguments that methodologically were vastly different from those proposed by their 'secular' classmates. For instance, students from religious educational institutions routinely cited a *hadith* (a statement of the Prophet Muhammad) or a verse from the Quran to support their point and were less prone to use examples from the historical experiences of societies outside the Muslim world (e.g. the conflict between Protestantism and Catholicism in Europe), whereas 'secular' students at both universities would defend their position with arguments taken from academic or religiously neutral sources. Intellectual cross-pollination among the students greatly enriched their learning experiences, making them more receptive to the position of the religious and cultural 'other', bridging the cognitive and experiential gap famously postulated by Edward Said (1994).

A key element of this exchange was the tension and opportunity provided by the so-called 'insider' and 'outsider' approaches to the study of Islam. We brought together different types of insiders: religious and 'ethnic' Muslims (those who come from a Muslim family but do not actively practice the religion), as well as different types of outsiders: students specializing in Islamic studies and other academic disciplines, e.g. cultural anthropology and political science.

Forcing the students to leave their ideological comfort zones, we designed a perspective-taking activity, asking the groups to articulate and defend the doctrinal positions of certain schools of thought and practice in Islam with which they may disagree or even consider 'heretical', e.g. those of the representatives of the rationalist Muʻtazilite theology or the doctrines of Muslim philosophers based on the 'pagan Greek wisdom' of Aristotelianism or Neo-Platonism.

This exercise was an eye-opener for both 'secular' and religious students, despite the initial discomfort and unease of the latter cohort, many members of which presented the positions assigned to them with such caveats as: "[s]ince I have to be the representative of the Muʻtazilite school today…" or "I personally do not think so, but because I am a representative of the Maliki school I would argue…".

Such cognitive challenges created a complex interactive environment in the classroom that is unique and unachievable otherwise. At SPbU, the 'secular' BA students developed close working relations with their *madrasa*-trained peers, as they helped each other in the areas they understood best. Muslim students helped their 'secular' classmates to master the intricacies of the Arabic language and traditional Muslim sciences (especially jurisprudence), whereas their 'secular' counterparts assisted their Muslim partners, who were less proficient in English and Western history and culture.

Regarding the international partnerships, the 'secular' SPbU BA students generally communicated better with their Michigan partners than their religious SPbU peers, perhaps due to their superior command of English. In more successful partnerships, instant communication tools were commonly used, e.g. WhatsApp. In less successful partnerships, the major problems cited were a lack (or lateness) of their partners' responses, the time difference, and the absence of initiative on either or both sides.

Chapter 7

4. Student feedback and lessons learned

While the use of written surveys provided comparability across courses, we found that many of the responses were terse to the point of being uninformative. Through personal interviews, we were able to collect a much broader range of useful feedback and have subsequently moved to using only interviews, conducted in both English and Russian by our instructional technologists.

Those students who recognized the value of the opportunity provided by the collaboration, unsurprisingly, reported getting the most out of the experience. The most successful cases led to new research directions that might otherwise have not been considered.

One Russian student identified the most illuminating moment of the exchange as when they received an email inquiring after their well-being in the wake of a terrorist attack in their city (Saint Petersburg). In the current tense political climate, the purely human aspects of the interactions and mutual understanding have an outsized effect.

Broader lessons were learned by the students about differing approaches to education and socialized classroom scripts (Belz & Müller-Hartmann, 2003). The Russian students expect expert-level knowledge from *anyone* who speaks up in the classroom and take the professor's statements at face value. American students are more eager to express their *own* conclusions from information they gather, even though they may potentially disagree with the professor. The lesson drawn by this contrast was described by one of the Russian students as learning "not to be afraid to think", which we see as a powerful expression of the value of this exchange.

We found that the small groups did not work consistently well for a host of reasons including availability, language, technology, and student viewpoint on their value. In future courses together, we plan to change the structure of the small group interactions to improve the quality and quantity. Tasks designed to require collaboration and student accountability will need to be re-examined as several students reported resorting to dividing the assignment among the members of the group without discussing it with one another. Adding reflective activities about the exchange will also prompt student thinking around learning from this experience.

In the all-group class discussions, students of both institutions indicated their appreciation for the engaging and challenging discussions that took place in the connected classroom. The challenges of engaging all the students regardless of their command of English and of providing balanced opportunities for all who wish to speak need more consideration in designing future courses of this nature.

5. Conclusion

Availing ourselves of the pedagogies and technologies of virtual exchange, we created two joint courses around the study of Islam, connecting students in Russia and the United States. We broadened the study of our subject area by including perspectives from different countries and religious and academic backgrounds through weekly joint discussions of course readings and small-group assignments outside of class. Students acquired expanded language and communication skills and were exposed to source material and educational approaches that they would have been unlikely otherwise to have encountered.

We, as instructors, are inspired to do more and look forward to other opportunities to connect our institutions in the future. We enjoyed the opportunity and challenge of creating and sustaining a close-knit textual and intellectual community driven by the common goals of discovering and testing various approaches to the conceptualization of Islam and its intellectual, moral-ethical, and cultural values and legacies. In the process, we learned how to deal effectively and impartially with multi-lingual, multi-denominational, and multi-cultural student contingents. Overall, in spite of the difficulties mentioned above, we consider these courses to be successful, and will be collaborating again in fall 2018 for the course 'Islam in/and Russia', adding Kazan Federal University to create a three-way collaboration.

Chapter 7

Acknowledgements

We would like to thank our respective universities, Saint Petersburg State University and the University of Michigan, for their support for these ongoing virtual exchange courses. The opportunity to create these valuable experiences for our students and our ability to meet and present this work at both the 2018 COIL and UNICollaboration conferences is greatly appreciated. Additionally, we extend our thanks to the two reviewers of this article for their very helpful feedback and suggestions.

References

Belz, J. A., & Müller-Hartmann, A. (2003). Teachers as intercultural learners: negotiating German–American telecollaboration along the institutional fault line. *The Modern Language Journal*, 87(1), 71-89. https://doi.org/10.1111/1540-4781.00179

Dorroll, C., Hall, K., & Baumi, D. (2019). On teaching Islam across cultures: virtual exchange pedagogy. In C. M. Dorroll (Ed.), *Teaching Islamic studies in the age of ISIS, islamophobia, and the Internet* (pp. 9-19). Indiana University Press. https://doi.org/10.2307/j.ctv9hvrmx.5

O'Dowd, R. (2018). From telecollaboration to virtual exchange: state-of-the-art and the role of UNICollaboration in moving forward. *Journal of Virtual Exchange*, *1*, 1-23. https://doi.org/10.14705/rpnet.2018.jve.1

O'Dowd, R., & Ware, P. (2009). Critical issues in telecollaborative task design. *Computer Assisted Language Learning*, 22(2), 173-188. https://doi.org/10.1080/09588220902778369

Said, E. W. (1994). Orientalism. Vintage Books.

8. Gamifying intercultural telecollaboration tasks for pre-mobility students

Marta Giralt[1] and Liam Murray[2]

Abstract

At a recent TeCoLa[3] project conference, Colpaert (2017) declared: "there is not enough evidence to suggest that technology has a direct effect on learning, not even virtual worlds. No, not even games… My hypothesis is… that the added value of technology depends on the designs of your learning environment on the one hand… and what I will talk about on task design on the other". This position paper argues that gamification may be effectively employed in engaging students' participation in pre-mobility preparation telecollaborative programmes, paying particular attention to environment and task design. Such preparation involves carrying out telecollaborative tasks with international partners and peers. Participation is voluntary and one of the biggest challenges in completing the set tasks results from the initial mismatch or 'non-fit' of pair partners. We present issues and ideas surrounding the possible gamification of task design in order to motivate students, to build an 'expectancy-value framework' (Dörnyei, 1998), and to remain engaged throughout the pre-mobility telecollaborative project.

Keywords: gamification, telecollaboration, motivation, tasks, pre-mobility students.

---

1. University of Limerick, Limerick, Ireland; marta.giralt@ul.ie

2. University of Limerick, Limerick, Ireland; liam.murray@ul.ie

3. Pedagogical Differentiation through Telecollaboration and Gaming for Intercultural and Content Integrated Language Teaching

How to cite this chapter: Giralt, M., & Murray, L. (2019). Gamifying intercultural telecollaboration tasks for pre-mobility students. In A. Turula, M. Kurek & T. Lewis (Eds), *Telecollaboration and virtual exchange across disciplines: in service of social inclusion and global citizenship* (pp. 65-71). Research-publishing.net. https://doi.org/10.14705/rpnet.2019.35.941

Chapter 8

1. Introduction

For more than 30 years, university students have participated in Study Abroad (SA) programmes as part of Erasmus or Erasmus+ initiatives. Availing of the SA opportunity has been very beneficial for undergraduate students. However, as mentioned elsewhere, some researchers, such as Byram and Dervin (2009), have shown that

> "while it is crucial to increase the opportunities for students to go abroad, it is erroneous to assume that students will automatically benefit from [their SA. Their research] highlights that it is [imperative] to prepare students for the mobility period so that they can fully benefit from their stay" (Giralt & Jeanneau, 2016, p. 2782).

Participating in telecollaboration projects that match students from the country where they are going to be travelling has been proven to be effective preparation for the period abroad (Giralt & Jeanneau, 2016). Nevertheless, the inclusion of such practices as part of the compulsory activities that students need to perform on their academic programmes could be difficult, and in many situations, they must be offered on a voluntary basis. For many years, the Intercultural Telecollaborative Language Learning (I-Tell) project, aimed at preparing students for their SA, has worked successfully in the University of Limerick. However, there have been some challenges: mismatch and asymmetries between the partners in terms of knowledge and needs, low motivation because of a lack of institutional reward, and issues with time management. As a result, there have been some low and non-completion rates, resulting in the students not maximising the opportunity to prepare better for their mobility programmes.

In this position paper, we propose gamifying the tasks that students must carry out during their Virtual Exchange (VE) in order to try to improve their engagement and persistence in completing the project. After justifying why we should gamify telecollaborative tasks, we provide an example of how this could be done.

2. Brief literature review on gamification

Gamification has been defined as the use of game design elements in non-game contexts, and is proven to be effective in motivating behavioural change and engaging learners to a high level (Buckley et al., 2018). In viewing game elements as "motivational affordances" (Deterding, 2011, p. 2), and establishing the relationship between these elements and motivational affordances, it is our contention that gamification may be successfully applied to improving the VE preparation tasks amongst would-be SA students.

It is clear that gamers may become highly engaged in their tasks and this has inevitably brought attention from other domains, including education. Everyday examples of this include organisations seeking to promote social and work changes (Oprescu, Jones, & Katsikitis, 2014) or groups creating games where players are solving an underlying problem – which is the essence of problem based learning – or through the creation of multifarious types of gamified educational websites (for many ideas on this topic, see Kapp, 2012).

Ferrara (2013) has argued that games "are able to contain and communicate persuasive messages" (p, 294). Whilst some researchers may see this as a negative phenomenon, where innocent game players are exploited by gamification designers (Bogost, 2011; Tulloch, 2014), Gee (2016) has argued that persuasion can be used for positive behavioural change as well. However, since its introduction, gamification has been dismissed as "pointsification", derided as "exploitationware", and labelled as an ephemeral "fad" (Ferrara, 2013, p. 289). Serious and professional game designers and researchers have tried to remove themselves from what they regard as simplistic renditions of elements that can be so very powerful in well-designed games. Alternatively, while many of these criticisms are invariably true, it would appear that something of a mind shift has transpired in the attitudes of game designers towards this concept. As "[g]amification is widely employed and disseminated in the corporate context" (Costa, Aparicio, Aparicio, & Aparicio, 2017, p. 64), we should be making a more systematic approach in integrating proven aspects of gamification. This approach may build upon and move beyond badges

(Griggio, 2018) and "soft certification" (Hauck & MacKinnon, 2016, p. 209), and seek to imitate and extend ambitious projects such as those delivered by Abruquah (2017). In doing so, we recognise the multifarious activities that occur within VE programmes, and it would be inappropriate for us to be prescriptive in our approach and with the several examples that we tentatively offer.

3. The why and how of gamified telecollaborative tasks

Our proposals for gamifying telecollaborative tasks are based on VE experience gathered over a four year period (2013-2017), with approximately 15 specialist and non-specialist language students per year participating. The participants consisted of students learning Spanish at the University of Limerick, Ireland, who went to Spain on Erasmus or work placements in Year 3, Semester 1 of their course. They were paired with students from the University of León and Universidad Autónoma de Madrid in Year 2, Semester 1. During the VE, all students had to conduct a series of telecollaborative tasks covering a range of intercultural topics (*introduction and the home university*; *finding out about the host country*; *expectations about living abroad*; *comparing university life and academic systems in the two countries*) during a period of eight weeks in the semester prior to their SA. The participants are advised to have two weekly exchanges with their international partner using e-mail or video-conferencing.

All participants had as intrinsic motivation the fact that they were going on Erasmus. However, that motivation was not enough to keep them engaged when mismatching or other challenges arose and sometimes they did not finalise the exchanges. A possible solution to help the more challenged students is to gamify the telecollaborative tasks. Our hypothesis is that in creating an 'expectancy-value framework' (Dörnyei, 1998), the extrinsic motivation emerging from the gamified tasks will engage students to the point that their motivation is re-ignited and helps them to complete all the tasks.

Our approach is to invite the students themselves to become 'game designers'. This consists of giving some suggestions of video game genres, e.g. adventure, role playing games, persuasive games, detective, and mini quests. These choices importantly introduce the idea of fun, creativity, freedom, collaboration, and the sense of community.

The task for the students is to be able to gamify the VE tasks. They will bring their experiences of gameplay from other games, digital or not, compose, and propose what *they* would consider to be authentic tasks for their peers, in negotiation with their facilitators.

We believe that the engagement will occur when students get involved in the game design (see Colpaert, 2017) and start mutually exploring, getting to know their virtual partner, their host, and local country. Our suggestions and examples about gamifying the telecollaborative tasks used in the VE I-Tell project would be based on our pedagogical practices and experience. These practices include working in the target language, reflecting on the target culture and completing appropriate tasks in reciprocal preparation for the SA (for a detailed description, see Giralt & Jeanneau, 2016). As a proposed example acting as an icebreaker exercise, the students might create an avatar to introduce themselves and get to know their partners. The students could become digital sojourners and collaboratively navigate a virtual world (e.g. Second Life) to discover the virtual partner university and its local culture. We will offer them tips, tricks, and gifting examples for them to develop and exploit in their gamified experience. Additional 'gamifiable' tasks could be and indeed should be identified by both students and facilitators. These tasks would inevitably be localised to their own VE environments. There are already multiple examples of task-based activities that use game elements in different language learning environments which could easily be incorporated into VEs. As a possible starting point we would recommend Purushotma, Thorne, and Wheatley's (2009) '10 Key Principles for Designing Video Games for Foreign Language Learning'. Finally, it would be important to introduce an informal sense of fun, allowing creativity to flow when students are creating their own tasks. Collaboration amongst the VE participants is key here.

4. Conclusion

In response to Colpaert's (2017) statement, we are proposing to flip the task and ask the students to use gaming elements and activities typically found in gaming to accomplish their VE tasks. This allows them to take ownership of the learning and exchange process, and to apply existing skills and knowledge whilst experiencing a mutually beneficial learning environment, maintaining their motivation and preparing effectively for their SA. The potential pitfalls could be many, and we should welcome and learn from them, of course, but this approach would attempt to introduce a greater investment from participants. When they invest their time, energy, and creativity and engage with the possible gamifiable elements, then the journey must surely be worth the risk. They may fail, but in gaming, as in learning, they may try again; "fail again, fail better" (Smith & Henriksen, 2016, p. 6).

References

Abruquah, E. (2017). *Effective telecollaboration in the digital age.* Paper presented at the Teoksessa TAMK-konferenssi - TAMK Conference 2017. Learning and working together. , Tampere: Tampereen ammattikorkeakoulu, Tampereen ammattikorkeakoulun julkaisuja.

Bogost, I. (2011). *Persuasive games: exploitationware.* Gamasutra. http://www.gamasutra.com/view/feature/6366/persuasive_games_exploitationware.php

Buckley, J., DeWille, T., Exton, C., Exton, G., & Murray, L. (2018). A gamification–motivation design framework for educational software developers. *Journal of Educational Technology Systems, 47*(1), 101-127. https://doi.org/10.1177/0047239518783153

Byram, M., & Dervin, F. (2009). *Students, staff and academic mobility in higher education.* Cambridge Scholars Publishing.

Colpaert, J. (2017). *Motivational aspects in task design for telecollaboration in challenging language learning contexts.* Paper presented at the Gamified Intercultural Telecollaboration for Foreign Language Learning Seminar, University of Roehampton. https://www.youtube.com/watch?v=cfO-jnvQmS8

Costa, C. J., Aparicio, M., Aparicio, S., & Aparicio, J. T. (2017). *Gamification usage ecology.* Paper presented at the Proceedings of the 35th ACM International Conference on the Design of Communication. https://doi.org/10.1145/3121113.3121205

Deterding, S. (2011). *Situated motivational affordances of game elements: a conceptual model.* Paper presented at the Gamification: Using game design elements in non-gaming contexts, a workshop at CHI.

Dörnyei, Z. (1998). Motivation in second and foreign language learning. *Language teaching, 31*(3), 117-135. https://doi.org/10.1017/S026144480001315X

Ferrara, J. (2013). Games for persuasion: argumentation, procedurality, and the lie of gamification. *Games and Culture, 8*(4), 289-304. https://doi.org/10.1177/1555412013496891

Gee, J. P. (2016). *Gaming lives in the twenty-first century: literate connections.* Springer.

Giralt, M., & Jeanneau, C. (2016). Preparing higher education language students for their period abroad through telecollaboration: The I-TELL Project. *AISHE-J: The All Ireland Journal of Teaching and Learning in Higher Education, 8*(2). http://ojs.aishe.org/index.php/aishe-j/article/view/278/440

Griggio, L. (2018). Linking virtual and physical mobility: a success story of a multilingual and multicultural exchange. *Sustainable Multilingualism, 12*(1), 88-112. https://doi.org/10.2478/sm-2018-0004

Hauck, M., & MacKinnon, T. (2016). A new approach to assessing online intercultural exchange. In R. O'Dowd & T. Lewis (Eds), *Online intercultural exchange: policy, pedagogy, practice* (pp. 209-232). Routledge.

Kapp, K. M. (2012). *The gamification of learning and instruction: game-based methods and strategies for training and education.* John Wiley & Sons.

Oprescu, F., Jones, C., & Katsikitis, M. (2014). I play at work—ten principles for transforming work processes through gamification. *Frontiers in psychology, 5*, 14, 1-5 https://doi.org/10.3389/fpsyg.2014.00014

Purushotma, R., Thorne, S., & Wheatley, J. (2009). *10 key principles for designing video games for foreign language learning.* https://pdxscholar.library.pdx.edu/wll_fac/9/

Smith, S., & Henriksen, D. (2016). Fail again, fail better: embracing failure as a paradigm for creative learning in the arts. *Art Education, 69*(2), 6-11. https://doi.org/10.1080/00043125.2016.1141644

Tulloch, R. (2014). Reconceptualising gamification: play and pedagogy. *Digital Culture & Education, 6*(4), 317-333.

9. A discussion on how teachers assess what foreign language students learn in telecollaboration

Suzi Marques Spatti Cavalari[1]

Abstract

Institutional integrated TeleTanDem (iiTTD) is a model of telecollaboration characterised as a series of tasks that are integrated into the syllabus of a foreign language course. This paper aims at presenting and discussing the assessment practice of a Brazilian teacher who integrated teletandem into her regular English as a Foreign Language (EFL) lessons within a teacher education programme. Among the different tasks that learners carry out within iiTTD, this study focusses on what is assessed by the teacher when offering formative feedback on learning diaries written by Brazilian participants. The study, of a qualitative interpretative nature, uses data collected by means of the tasks that 13 Brazilian learners carried out within iiTTD in 2017. Results show that the teacher was able to assess (1) students' self-assessment skills, (2) language accuracy (when diaries are written in English), (3) the learning of content presented in class, and (4) intercultural issues that may emerge during teletandem oral sessions.

Keywords: foreign language learning, teacher's assessment, telecollaboration.

---

1. Universidade Estadual Paulista (UNESP), São José do Rio Preto, Brazil; smscavalari@gmail.com

How to cite this chapter: Cavalari, S. M. S. (2019). A discussion on how teachers assess what foreign language students learn in telecollaboration. In A. Turula, M. Kurek & T. Lewis (Eds), *Telecollaboration and virtual exchange across disciplines: in service of social inclusion and global citizenship* (pp. 73-79). Research-publishing.net. https://doi.org/10.14705/rpnet.2019.35.942

Chapter 9

1. Introduction: telecollaboration and assessment

Teletandem (Telles, 2006) is a model of telecollaboration which is based on the tandem principles (autonomy, reciprocity, bilingualism) and has been carried out at Universidade Estadual Paulista (UNESP), in Brazil. iiTTD is a specific model of teletandem that is characterised by Cavalari and Aranha (2016) as a series of tasks that are embedded in language courses so that teletandem practice can both feed and be fed by regular foreign language lessons. The tasks learners are expected to carry out in iiTTD are: (1) participating in teletandem oral sessions, (2) writing learning diaries, (3) answering initial and post-questionnaires, and (4) writing collaboratively. In accordance with studies on telecollaborative practice (Lewis & Walker, 2003; Little & Brammerts, 1996; O'Rourke, 2007), Cavalari and Aranha (2016) point out that there are three key pedagogical procedures to meaningful integration: (1) preparing learners for autonomous collaborative learning, (2) blending virtual exchanges into classroom activities by means of integrating tasks, and (3) considering different assessment perspectives (the teacher's, the learner's, the peer's).

Despite a considerable body of research on peer feedback and self-assessment, which demonstrated that they can be driving forces in telecollaborative learning, there seems to be a dearth of investigations on assessment practices. O'Dowd (2010) carried out a comprehensive study on assessment of online activities (including virtual exchanges). The study showed that teachers tended to focus their assessment on (1) participation (the number of times students send emails or post messages in forums, for example), (2) ability to interact with others and develop positive relationships, and (3) intercultural communicative competence. The author also discussed some assessment practices (use of grading rubrics and portfolios) which involved both a formative (process-based) approach, which is particularly suited to assessing telecollaborative learning, and a summative (product-based) perspective, which reflects institutional demands. He remarked that it is crucial to develop comprehensive models for assessing online language activity which include the skills, attitudes and literacies that educators claim are involved in telecollaborative projects.

In this paper, we focus on the formative aspect of assessment and investigate the feedback offered by a teacher on learners' diaries in iiTTD. Considering that diaries are written with the purpose of developing autonomous learning, this study aims at discussing what teachers may assess by means of this task.

2. Methodology

This is a case study that focusses on a Brazilian teacher's assessment practice as she gave feedback on her students' learning diaries within iiTTD. Telecollaboration was integrated into the second year of an English as a foreign language course taught within a four-year teacher education major. The tasks which students carried out during the eight week telecollaborative project were: (1) participating in six synchronous oral sessions (via Skype), (2) writing six learning diary entries, (3) writing two texts in English and sharing them with the teletandem partner, (4) revising two of their partner's texts in Portuguese, and (5) answering two questionnaires (initial and final). Analysis is based on data collected by means of the diaries written by 13 Brazilian students between March and April, 2017. Students could choose whether to write their diaries in English or in Portuguese: eight decided to write in English and five, in Portuguese. Diaries were written in Google Docs and shared with the teacher by means of Google Drive. The focus of the analysis is on the aspects attended to by the teacher as she offered feedback to each student's diary entry on a weekly basis. The analysis of the teacher's feedback was based on the categories proposed by O'Dowd (2010), but it also took into consideration the emergence of new categories.

3. Results and discussion

Data analysis revealed that most feedback offered by the teacher focussed on aspects of autonomous learning and self-assessment. When learners vaguely mentioned what they had learned, the teacher asked them to be more specific, encouraging reflection and monitoring.

Figure 1. Fragment 1 (teacher's comment, Diary 2, Participant 11)

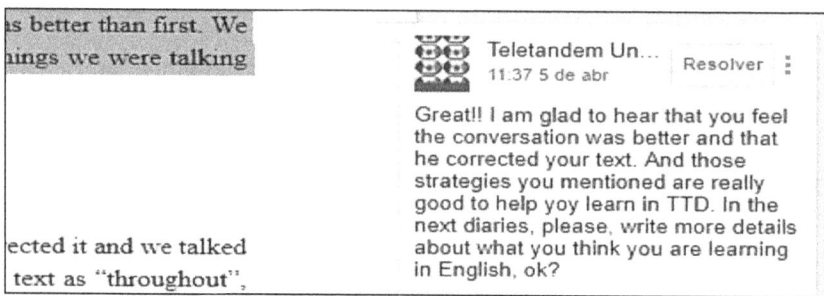

The fragment in Figure 1 shows that the feedback also focussed on the use of learning strategies, prompting the student to realise that the strategies he used were appropriate for learning in telecollaboration and assisting him in using other strategies. This is evidence that diaries are serving their purpose of promoting reflection on learning and developing autonomy, but, more importantly, it is evidence that, from a formative perspective, diaries are a powerful assessment instrument for teachers.

There was also strong evidence that the teacher's feedback had a focus on students' motivation and feelings towards learning in iiTTD. The fragment Figure 2 shows a comment the teacher made as a student mentioned how disappointed he was about his English performance during the oral session.

Figure 2. Fragment 2 (teacher's comment, Diary 4, Participant 2)

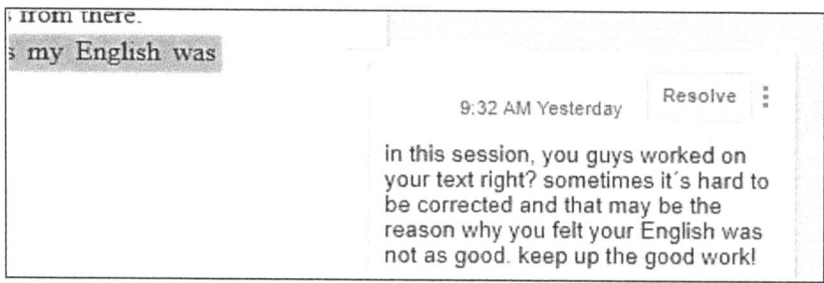

The teacher's comment is reassuring and may help the learner save face and maintain a positive attitude towards telecollaborative practice. This seems to be crucial in assisting students in coping with the role that social relationships and affective factors play in any learning context, but particularly in online intercultural exchanges.

Another focus of this teacher's feedback was on language accuracy. When the diaries were written in English, the teacher changed the colour of some words (or stretches of text) and added comments to give further information about inappropriate words or expressions. In Fragment 3, instead of using the comment feature of Google docs, the teacher left a comment highlighted with a different colour in the end of the diary entry:

> **Fragment 3.** "the words marked in blue are my 'tips' about how you can improve your text. Let's talk about the problems you had with the 'application letter' in class, ok? 😊" (teacher's comment, Diary 1, Participant 6).

Considering the diary is a private text intended to foster reflection on the learning process, it seems crucial that the teacher does not correct the linguistic items she finds inappropriate, leaving space for learners' decisions on what, if anything, they want to change in their texts. As to the 'application letter', which was one of the texts Brazilian learners wrote and shared with their partners, this student mentioned in her diary that she found her partner's revision contradictory in relation to what she had learned in class. The teacher's comment indicates that telecollaboration can furnish meaningful content for discussion in the classroom.

Finally, data suggested that this teacher's assessment focussed on intercultural issues (see Figure 3). In this fragment, the student wrote, in Portuguese, that he and his partner discussed the impeachment of Dilma Roussef (the former Brazilian president) as well as the policies of Donald Trump (the current American president). The teacher's feedback highlighted the fact that those are complex topics to be discussed in the foreign language and asked the student what he had learned about political issues both in Brazil and in the USA.

Figure 3. Fragment 4 (teacher's comment, Diary 4, Participant 7)

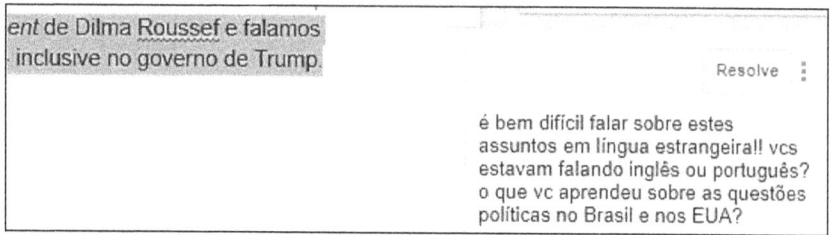

4. Conclusion

Data analysis revealed that the teacher's feedback focussed on aspects of autonomous learning (students' self-assessment of their language learning), attitudes and affective factors (social aspects of language learning), language accuracy (when diaries are written in English), and (inter)cultural issues. These results suggest that teachers' assessments of learner diaries may embrace individual and social aspects of telecollaborative learning as well as its linguistic and cultural contents. The results corroborate some of O'Dowd's (2010) findings if we acknowledge that when teachers assess ability to communicate with others and intercultural communicative competence, they are dealing with social, affective, and cultural issues. However, this study also offers evidence that, from a formative perspective, teacher assessment involves aspects of autonomous learning that are intertwined with classroom teaching.

References

Cavalari, S. M. S., & Aranha, S. (2016). Teletandem: integrating e-learning into the foreign language classroom. *Acta Scientiarum: Language and Culture, 38*(4), 327-336. https://doi.org/10.4025/actascilangcult.v38i4.28139

Lewis, T., & Walker, L. (Eds). (2003). *Autonomous language learning in tandem.* Academy Electronic Publications.

Little, D., & Brammerts, H. (1996). *A guide to language learning in tandem via the internet.* CLCS Occasional Paper 46. Trinity College, Centre for Language and Communication Studies.

O'Dowd, R. (2010). Issues in the assessment of online interaction and exchange. *Telecollaboration, 2*, 337-360.

O'Rourke, B. (2007). Models of telecollaboration: e(tandem). In R. O'Dowd (Ed.), *Online intercultural exchange: an introduction for foreign language teachers* (pp. 41-62). Multilingual Matters. https://doi.org/10.21832/9781847690104-005

Telles, J. A. (2006). *Teletandem Brasil: línguas estrangeiras para todos.* Research Project, Universidade Estadual Paulista.

10 The Global Virtual Teams Project: learning to manage team dynamics in virtual exchange

Rachel Lindner[1] and Dónal O'Brien[2]

Abstract

Our paper positions telecollaboration in the business context, in which culturally, geographically, temporally, and functionally dispersed teams – so-called Global Virtual Teams (GVTs) – are increasingly being used to engage an organisation's creative and problem-solving capabilities. In this virtual workplace, team members must complete tasks efficiently, despite language and cultural difference, geographical distance, technological complexity, and variance in organisational goals. We propose that virtual exchange projects can provide students with valuable pre-workplace experience of the demands placed on GVTs and the skills needed to operate successfully in a GVT environment. The GVTs Project outlined in our paper was set up for this purpose, and is run across five business schools by management and ESP teachers. We identify themes that have emerged through project observation and student reports, and exemplify how students manage the challenges of working in a GVT with a case study in which a project participant analyses her team's dynamics[3].

Keywords: Global Virtual Teams, global factories, interdisciplinary virtual exchange, management and communication skills.

---

1. University of Paderborn, Paderborn, Germany; rachel.lindner@uni-paderborn.de

2. Dublin City University Business School, Dublin, Ireland; donal.obrien@dcu.ie

3. We would like to thank Katharina Sander of the University of Paderborn whose team analysis has been used for the case study.

How to cite this chapter: Lindner, R., & O'Brien, D. (2019). The Global Virtual Teams Project: learning to manage team dynamics in virtual exchange. In A. Turula, M. Kurek & T. Lewis (Eds), *Telecollaboration and virtual exchange across disciplines: in service of social inclusion and global citizenship* (pp. 81-89). Research-publishing.net. https://doi.org/10.14705/rpnet.2019.35.943

Chapter 10

1. Introduction

The modern manager needs to work with greater creativity and flexibility in today's diverse and digitally enhanced work environment. Rapid technological progress and access to new markets have driven multinational corporations to create more complex, fluid, and interdependent company structures, which Buckley (2009) conceptualises as *global factories*. Within these firms there is a major focus on offshoring and outsourcing certain activities, and building competencies within the organisation and with external partners in key areas. These developments have given rise to the implementation of GVTs, defined by Daim et al. (2012) as "culturally diverse, geographically dispersed, electronically communicating workgroups" (p. 199). It is these teams that are being used to engage an organisation's creative, knowledge-sharing, and problem-solving capabilities across borders.

GVT-work is reputedly challenging, and research draws attention to the skills needed to collaborate on delivering project outputs despite language barriers and cultural diversity, geographical distance, technological complexity, and different organisational goals (Gilson et al., 2015). However, there are just a handful of reported examples of pedagogy aimed at preparing business students for these work scenarios (including Osland et al., 2004, and Taras et al., 2013), indicating a lack of such skills training in tertiary education. In this paper, we describe a learning environment which we have designed to help students acquire the experience and develop the skill sets needed to become drivers of best GVT practice. We outline the project experience of one team, highlighting themes that are recurrent in our project observations and drawing parallels with the literature on GVTs from the fields of business and management.

2. The project

The GVTs Project was initiated five years ago and combines insights from business studies of GVTs with research into telecollaboration to provide students with an insider experience of working in a GVT. The 2017 iteration had 142 participants from the Business and Economics faculties of Dublin City University in Ireland, Masaryk Institute of Advanced Studies in Prague, Masaryk University in Brno in the Czech Republic, the University of Paderborn in Germany, and Tampere University of Applied Sciences in Finland. The project is embedded in a blended learning course, with classroom sessions at participating institutions dedicated to subject input, familiarising participants with aspects of working in GVTs through study and discussion of literature in the field, project-relevant language skills development and reflection on the learning experience.

In order to simulate real-life GVTs, participants are organised into teams with four to five members that are diverse not only in terms of national and institutional culture, but also by gender, language proficiency, academic maturity, age, and work experience. Also in keeping with GVTs, deadlines are purposefully tight. Teams have just eight weeks to conduct team-building and then negotiate, research, and present a project in which they compare a product, service, or business procedure across at least two different cultures (see Figure 1).

Figure 1. Project phases

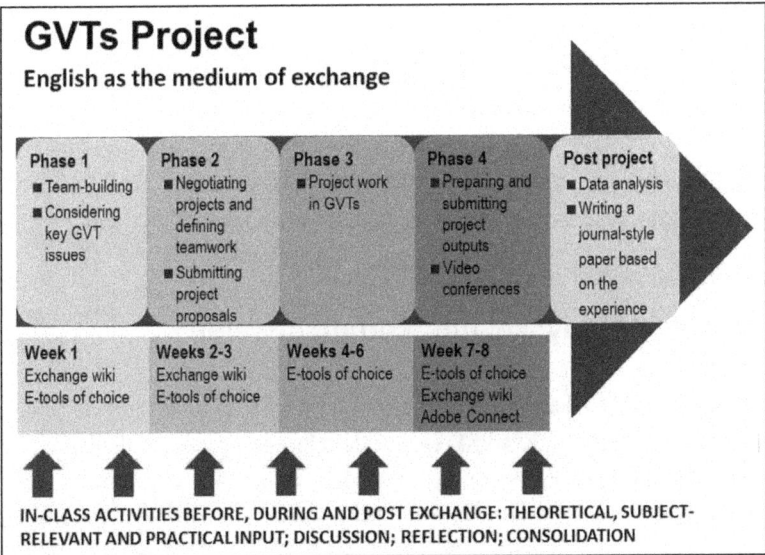

3. Individual team analysis

During the project, students archive communications in all media channels they use and keep a diary of the project from their insider perspective, logging any critical incidents. After the project, they analyse the data they collected quantitatively. This involves temporal analysis of the quantity, distribution, and frequency of communication over time in the different media. The temporal analysis is mapped on to the type of communication, e.g. whether transactional or interpersonal, whether it is about content, administrative issues, socialising, or conflict-management. Students then analyse this data qualitatively in relation to the literature on GVTs, identifying and comparing their own experience with research from the field. Each of these analyses represents an insider case study of a student GVT. Although students touch on a range of themes, the four most frequently occurring are

- leadership,
- impact of mediated communication,
- trust, and
- commitment/motivation.

The following case study of one of the project teams has been chosen to exemplify how these themes manifest themselves in team dynamics.

4. Case study: results and discussion

The team described here was diverse in terms of national and institutional affiliations (German, Irish, and French, whereby the French student was doing an Erasmus semester in Brno), age (ranging from 19-26), gender, academic maturity (from 3rd semester bachelor to 3rd semester master's degree), and English language skills (from B2 learner to native speaker). The analysis foregrounds the impact of communication behaviours, trust, and commitment on the emergence of a leader.

4.1. Emergent leadership

According to Gibson and Cohen (2003) it is not common practice for companies to assign leadership to a GVT member. Instead, leaders tend to emerge due to behaviours such as proactivity, commitment, expertise, or managerial skills. Furthermore, literature on GVTs (e.g. Panteli & Tucker, 2009) shows that more than one leader may emerge during the lifetime of a GVT, depending on the competences required for different project phases. By analysing the trajectory of the GVT in question, tipping points can be identified, which Boyatzis (2008) defines as moments when a group leader emerges due to certain behaviours. As team members became more aware of each other's competences, one student became the team manager, while others were perceived to be leaders in other areas of expertise, for example as report editor or presentation moderator. Notably, due to the temporary nature of GVTs and the limited knowledge that team members have of one another, leadership qualities are perceived through online communication of those qualities. Leaders therefore often emerge due to their communication behaviours.

4.2. Impact of mediated communication

Strong 'telepresence' is often a sign of an emergent GVT leader, and is expressed through the quantity and the quality of communication, in interaction initiation and speed of response (Zigurs, 2003). The German team participant was the most proactive, prolific, reliable, and responsive communicator. Her telepresence was firstly demonstrated as the creator of the WhatsApp group and initiator of most conversations. Not only did she write the most communications, but her average message length was also the longest (Figure 2).

In team video conferences, although attendance was good overall, only she attended all conferences from start to finish, demonstrating reliability and commitment to the project, and thereby inspiring trust in other team members.

Chapter 10

Figure 2. **Left**: number of WhatsApp messages per WhatsApp member per week. **Right**: average number of words per message per member (f=female; m=male; TM=team member; C, I, G=Czech, Irish, German)[4]

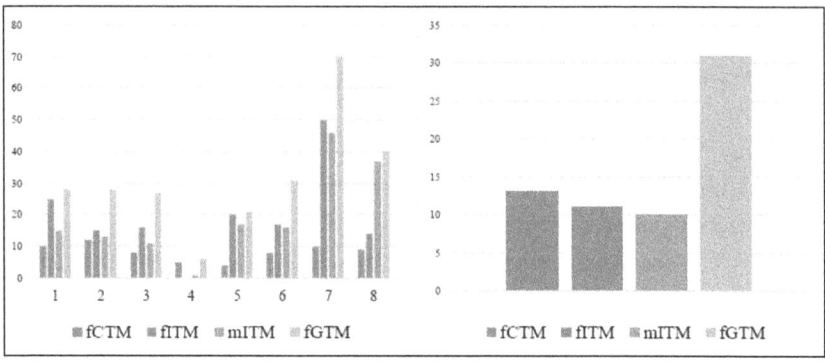

4.3. Trust

Tyran, Tyran, and Shepherd (2003) found what McAllister (1995) refers to as 'role performance trust' to have a strong impact on leadership development. Role performance trust develops when members demonstrate competencies needed to accomplish a task. The German team member's communication skills led to her becoming the team manager. This may have been compounded by the fact that she was the oldest member of the group, close to completing her master's degree and had excellent English skills. However, different team members also inspired trust in their ability to perform roles competently, leading to a distribution of leadership. Irrespective of leadership, however, the team members inspired trust in each other through their overall online visibility and engagement throughout the project.

4.4. Motivation and commitment

Asymmetries in motivation and commitment are problematic in telecollaboration and real-life GVTs alike. Team members frequently work on parallel projects,

---

4. Figure 2 is reproduced here by kind permission of Katharina Sander.

and tend to prioritise face-to-face projects due to their visibility. This brings us back to the concept of telepresence and its impact not only on emergent leadership, but on team dynamics as a whole. In our experience, teams who met regularly in video conferences seemed to be more satisfied with their teams, irrespective of measurable project success, as was true of the case study GVT. This shores up our belief that video conferencing, and video conferencing skills development, should ideally be a mandatory part of the project, even if participants find scheduling difficult.

5. Conclusion

Research into GVTs has highlighted that for all the benefits that GVTs can bring to organisations, there are massive challenges in dealing with people across cultural and technological distance and organisations (Ferrazzi, 2014). Multinational organisations are discovering that to realise the benefits of GVTs, participants need more specific skills training. Telecollaboration projects can play an important preparatory role here, but research is needed to pinpoint those skills.

The student who contributed her team analysis for our case study summarised her experience as follows:

> "It gave us the possibility to gain deep insights on how to leverage the advantages of multifaceted abilities that exist within a randomly-formed team... how to cope with problems that arise from cultural differences, varying language skills and global dispersion... The project helped me to evaluate my own communication and leadership skills and I learned that I must reveal my train of thought more extensively for the other team members to be able to follow my ideas more easily".

These are important insights, both for the student and for us. Her insider analysis helps us to understand the impact on team dynamics of the four themes we identified – leadership, online communication, trust, and commitment/ motivation. This is a line of research that is worth pursuing more systematically in future iterations of the GVTs Project. By analysing the interplay of these themes across a number of team constellations, we might be able to determine more precisely which skills are needed to deal with the challenges of virtual, international teamwork and how to foster them in the design of our project.

References

Boyatzis, R. E. (2008). Leadership development from a complexity perspective. *Consulting Psychology Journal: Practice and Research, 60*(4), 44-56. https://doi.org/10.1037/1065-9293.60.4.298

Buckley, P. J. (2009). Internalisation thinking: from the multinational enterprise to the global factory. *International Business Review, 18*(3), 224-235. https://doi.org/10.1016/j.ibusrev.2009.01.006

Daim, T. U., Ha, A., Reutiman, S., Hughes, B., Pathak, U., Bynum, W., & Bhatla, A. (2012). Exploring the communication breakdown in global virtual teams. *International Journal of Project Management, 30*(2), 199-212. https://doi.org/10.1016/j.ijproman.2011.06.004

Ferrazzi, K. (2014). Managing yourself. *Harvard Business Review, 92*(12), 120-123.

Gibson, C. B., & Cohen, S. (2003). *Virtual teams that work: creating conditions for virtual effectiveness*. Jossey-Bass.

Gilson, L. L., Maynard, M. T., Jones Young, N. C., Vartiainen, M., & Hakonen, M. (2015). Virtual teams research: 10 years, 10 themes, and 10 opportunities. *Journal of Management, 41*(5), 1313-1337. https://doi.org/10.1177/0149206314559946

McAllister, D. J. (1995). Affect and cognition-based trust as foundations for interpersonal cooperation in organisations. *The Academy of Management Journal, 38*(1), 24-59.

Osland, J., Bird, A., Scholz, C., Maznevski, M., McNett, J., Mendenhall, M., Stein, V., & Weyer, D. (2004). Global reality with virtual teams: lessons from the globally distant virtual teams project. In C. Wankel & R. Defillippi (Eds), *The cutting edge of international management education* (pp. 115-141). Information Age Publishing.

Panteli, N., & Tucker, R. (2009). Power and trust in global virtual teams. *Communications of the ACM, 52*(12), 113-115. https://doi.org/10.1145/1610252.1610282

Taras, V., Caprar, D., Rottig, D., Sarala, R., Zakaria, N., Zhao, F., Jiménez, A., Wankel, C., Lei, W., Minor, M., Bryla, P., Ordenana, X., Bode, A., Schuster, A., Vaiginiene, E., Froese, F., Bathula, H., Yajnik, N., Baldegger, R., & Huang, V. (2013). A global classroom? Evaluating the effectiveness of global virtual collaboration as a teaching tool in management education. *Academy of Management Learning & Education, 12*(3), 414-435. https://doi.org/10.5465/amle.2012.0195

Tyran, K. L., Tyran, C. K., & Shepherd, M. (2003). Exploring emerging leadership in virtual teams. In C.B. Gibson & S.G. Cohen (Eds), *Virtual teams that work: creating conditions for virtual effectiveness* (pp. 183-195). Jossey-Bass.

Zigurs, I. (2003). Leadership in virtual teams: oxymoron or opportunity? *Organisational dynamics, 31*(4), 339-351. https://doi.org/10.1016/S0090-2616(02)00132-8

11. Virtual exchange across disciplines: telecollaboration and the question of asymmetrical task design

Martin Štefl[1]

Abstract

This paper discusses an experience with an asymmetric online intercultural exchange between three different groups of students which took place during a specialised soft skills-focussed language class of Business Networking in English (BNiE) at the MIAS School of Business, Czech Technical University, Prague (MIAS). The results of the post-project discussion and perceptions of MIAS students participating in the asymmetric telecollaboration are analysed and conclusions are drawn.

Keywords: telecollaboration, task design, symmetry, and asymmetry.

1. Introduction

The growing importance of combining content and language teaching in higher education poses new challenges to course and task design. One of the most acute questions is how to successfully incorporate Online Intercultural Exchange (OIE) into specialised language courses which focus on developing specific soft and/or transversal skills. It is often the case that introducing OIE into such courses would be clearly in line with the aims of the given course, yet finding a suitable OIE partner with perfectly symmetrical pedagogical aims

---

1. Czech Technical University, Prague, Czech Republic; martin.stefl@cvut.cz

How to cite this chapter: Štefl, M. (2019). Virtual exchange across disciplines: telecollaboration and the question of asymmetrical task design. In A. Turula, M. Kurek & T. Lewis (Eds), *Telecollaboration and virtual exchange across disciplines: in service of social inclusion and global citizenship* (pp. 91-97). Research-publishing.net. https://doi.org/10.14705/rpnet.2019.35.944

might prove rather difficult. Although it has been argued that OIEs are never entirely symmetric (Loizidou & Mangenot, 2016, p. 155) and various forms of asymmetry, e.g. the asymmetry of student/institutional status, students' language and/or other skills, motivation, prior knowledge, needs, or class/group size and heterogeneity (Wigham, Mayer, & Fumagalli, 2014, p. 3), exist in all OIEs, course designers should always pay close attention to any asymmetries that threaten to negatively impact the outcome of the OIE. An asymmetry which can easily put at risk the outcome of an OIE is the asymmetry of workload. This asymmetry played an important role in the discussed three way OIE between the students of a specialised Bachelor of Science (BSc) course of BNiE at the MIAS, students of English for special purposes from École Nationale Supérieure de Chimie, de Biologie, et de Physique, Bordeaux (French partner), and students of Business English from Budapest Business School (Hungarian partner)[2].

Business networking is an umbrella term which describes "the creation and use of personal contacts for one's own benefit or for the benefit of the group" (Jenkins, 2003, p. 65), including "the process of creating, cultivating, and capitalising on trust-based, mutually beneficial relationships" (Baber, Waymon, Alphonso, & Wylde, 2015, p. 22). Elaborating on this definition, Sharma and Barrett (2010, p. 7) describe a good networker as a competent communicator with solid vocabulary, grammar, and cultural awareness, and good command of communication strategies and interaction patterns. In addition to this, competent networkers are said to be capable of "educating their contacts" about who they are, what they do, and what they have to offer (Graham, 2012, p. 26).

The need to expose advanced BNiE students to cognitively stimulating real-life networking situations which would allow for systematic development of the above defined skills led to the idea of constructing the NiE curriculum

---

2. Credentials: The original idea of the project was conceptualised during an 'Intercultural Skills for the Language Classroom' and 'Telecollaboration and Virtual Exchange in Education' training at the University of León, Spain, in February 2016 (ICCAGE funded by Erasmus+ KA2 Programme No 2015-1-CZ01-KA203-013992) by Eva Bartane Varga of Budapest Business School, Hungary, and the author of this paper. First implementation: Réka Asztalos from BBS. BNiE implementation: Erika Huszár and Anita Theodóra Wiesenmayer from Budapest Business School, Hungary, and Mireille Lamarque and Claudia Brosnahan from École Nationale Supérieure de Chimie, de Biologie, et de Physique.

around an OIE based on "student-centred, collaborative approaches to learning where knowledge and understanding are constructed through interaction and negotiation" (O'Dowd, 2016, p. 292). Given the fact that telecollaborative tasks involving "different linguistic and cultural communities [...] have a strong possibility of producing negotiation of meaning" (O'Dowd & Waire, 2009, pp. 174-175), the course designers decided to modify an OIE, which was in previous years implemented symmetrically (i.e. with only one partner), by expanding it to a cooperation with two different international partners. The rationale behind this decision was that the comparison of results achieved in cooperation with Hungarian and French partners would allow for knowledge being constructed through a contrast between different experiences rather than being simply transmitted by one partner and/or directly by the teacher. In addition to this, this approach provided individuals with more space to pursue their specific pedagogical aims, e.g. differentiate the amount of workload the students can devote to the project as part of the given course and focus on a different project output, while mutually benefitting from an OIE.

2. The online exchange

Given this situation, the BNiE syllabus was built around a synchronous OIE[3] focussing on training and development of personal and interpersonal skills, team-work, business communication, and networking routines. The nine week OIE, which took place from March to May 2018, comprised of a series of online encounters simulating the launch of a fictional product onto the international partner's market. Importantly, from the perspective of MIAS students, the project ran in two parallel lines: MIAS students cooperated with their French and Hungarian partners while these two partners were, given their specific educational aims and the role of the OIE in their course, not in touch during the project. This situation created the task and workload asymmetry between MIAS students and their international partners.

---

3. For the full description of this original project module entitled 'Negotiating with International Partners', see ICCAGE (2017, pp. 125-154).

Chapter 11

Table 1 below describes individual project tasks, detailing the two project lines which the MIAS students had to accomplish in cooperation with their Hungarian and French partners.

Table 1. Project tasks table

	Hungarian Branch	French Branch
1.	Chose a product you will export to your partner's market, consider you product strategy, product description, product marketing materials, etc.	
2.	Get in touch with your Hungarian partner.	Get in touch with your French partner.
3.	E-mail a product description and questionnaire about your partner's market in relation to your product to your Hungarian partner.	E-mail a product description and questionnaire about your partner's market in relation to your product to your French partner.
4.	Answer the Hungarian partner's questionnaire.	Answer the French partner's questionnaire.
5.	Change your product description, strategy, etc., based on your partner's feedback.	Change your product description, strategy, etc., based on your partner's feedback.
6.	E-mail your preliminary quotation.	Shoot a video pitch.
7.	Skype negotiation.	Watch and evaluate partner's video pitches.
8.	Follow-up e-mail and minutes.	Share feedback on your partner's video pitches.

For MIAS students, the asymmetry in workload was compensated for by the fact that the "information exchange" (O'Dowd & Waire, 2009, p. 175) tasks 1-5 were analogical in both project lines. First, MIAS students chose a product to export, developed a cohesive product strategy and description, and then exchanged information about the product and target market with their respective partners. Based on their partner's feedback, students adjusted their product description/strategy to suit the specifics of the French and/or Hungarian market. Their partners followed the same procedure, however, did not work with two partners at the same time. The final outcome of the French project line was a product video pitch followed-up by feedback activities; the outcome of the Hungarian part was a simulated Skype negotiation in which two student teams pretended to be importers/exporters of their respective products and attempted to negotiate the best contract. The negotiation was concluded by a follow-up e-mail summarising the details of the contract and negotiation minutes.

3. Method and results

To decide on the feasibility of the asymmetrical arrangement of the project, which was two years previously implemented symmetrically, the MIAS teacher decided to run a simple post-project survey among involved MIAS students, and organise focus group discussions. The survey comprised of 16 questions addressing various aspects of the project; 13 were five point Likert scale questions and three were open ended questions. Question 11 focussed on the project workload asymmetry and asked students to express their (dis-)agreement with the statement: "International students I cooperate with are assigned the same amount of work as part of the project as me/my team". Out of 32 participating students, 18 chose to 'fully agree', 10 chose 'agree', and 4 preferred 'undecided'; options 'disagree' and 'fully disagree' were not selected.

The results, however, contrasted with answers provided in open-ended question 15, which asked students to name the main problems they experienced during the project. Despite generally perceiving the project as successful and beneficial in terms of developing their real-life networking skills, students reported the following problems: (1) problems in communication, mainly their partners' (un-)willingness to meet deadlines (22/32), (2) their partners' unwillingness to keep the project on a formal level (21/32), (3) problems caused by the institutional setting (21/32), and (4) telecollaborative task scheduling (18/32); interestingly, none of the responses spontaneously pointed out problems with task/workload asymmetry. This was confirmed during focus group discussions where students admitted that the biggest frustration was the lack of fast-enough and/or appropriate responses from the partner team (Problems 1, 2, and 4 above) affecting their ability to meet project deadlines, as well as the fact that the project took place during the final semester of their studies and took away time they would have otherwise spent writing their thesis (Problem 3 above).

4. Discussion

Despite the limited scope of the survey, the given answers make it safe to assume that the encountered problems are to be attributed to the micro-asymmetry between the cooperating student teams rather than to the macro-asymmetry of the project design and task sequencing in general. When inquired directly, students naturally did not see the workload asymmetry as something desirable, but at the same time did not see it as an impediment to successful completion of the project.

The phenomena of micro/macro-asymmetry are naturally linked, however, it might be argued that in the case of this particular project, the organisational and communicational problems might have appeared due to an asymmetry of student/teacher expectations rather than as a result of the quantitative asymmetry in workload. Although the workload asymmetry was not perceived as desirable per se, it seems not to have been mentioned as a problem simply because it was something the students could deal with on their own; in other words it was something that, unlike the need to rely on their international partners, was not 'beyond the student's control', and thus did not prevent the students from completing the project. From this perspective, the asymmetry in workload did not significantly influence the project outcome.

5. Conclusion

As various asymmetries naturally exist in most OIE projects, OIE designers should not automatically perceive them as factors negatively influencing the outcome of their OIE. The experience drawn from this project, however specific to the given context and limited by the number of student responses, suggests that OIE designers should carefully distinguish between different asymmetries and draw from past experience in order to anticipate which asymmetries might impede the project and which might be productively embodied into the project design. At all times it is crucial that all relevant project asymmetries should be carefully explained to involved students.

References

Baber, A., Waymon, L., Alphonso A., Wylde, J. (2015). *Strategic connections: the new face of networking in a collaborative world*. American Management Association.

Graham, A. (2012). *Business relationships: personal branding and profitable networking made easy*. John Wiley & Sons.

ICCAGE. (2017). *Intercultural communicative competence: open educational resource*. http://docs.wixstatic.com/ugd/526a9b_63716cfeea1d4a12ba81bfb7d6a47ea1.pdf

Jenkins, D. (2003). *Networking and sharing information*. Pergamon Flexible Learning.

Loizidou, D., & Mangenot, F. (2016). Interactional dimension of online asynchronous exchange in an asymmetric telecollaboration. In S. Jager, M. Kurek & B. O'Rourke (Eds), *New directions in telecollaborative research and practice: selected papers from the second conference on telecollaboration in higher education* (pp. 155-161). https://doi.org/10.14705/rpnet.2016.telecollab2016.502

O'Dowd, R. (2016). Emerging trends and new directions in telecollaborative learning. *Calico Journal, 33*(3), 291-310. https://doi.org/10.1558/cj.v33i3.30747

O'Dowd, R., & Waire, P. (2009). Critical issues in telecollaborative task design. *Computer Assisted Language Learning, 22*(2), 173-188. https://doi.org/10.1080/09588220902778369

Sharma, P., & Barrett, B. (2010). *Business networking in English*. Macmillan.

Wigham, C. R., Mayer, H., & Fumagalli, M. (2014). *An asymmetrical telecollaborative project and the evolution of its learning design: the Université Blaise Pascal - London School of Economics experience*. Telecollaboration in University Foreign Language Education, Léon, Spain. https://edutice.archives-ouvertes.fr/edutice-00877553

12. A proposal to study the links between the sociocultural and the linguistic dimensions of eTandem interactions

Marco Cappellini[1]

Abstract

After identifying a major limitation of current research on telecollaboration, I propose to develop a methodological framework to empirically study the link between the sociocultural dimension and the linguistic dimension of interaction in eTandem via desktop videoconferencing. For the sociocultural dimension, I study which roles the learners take during the interactions using discourse analysis tools. For the linguistic dimension, I focus mainly on different types of conversational side sequences identified in the francophone interactionist literature. In the end, I discuss the relevance that the methodological framework I propose can have for research on telecollaboration and point to studies that explored this avenue.

Keywords: research paradigm, conversation analysis, corpus analysis, eTandem, dynamic complex systems theory.

1. Introduction

Studies of telecollaboration almost exclusively focus on only one project, which prevents researchers from comparing projects and establishing

---

1. Aix Marseille University, CNRS, LPL, Aix-en-Provence, France; marco.cappellini@univ-amu.fr

How to cite this chapter: Cappellini, M. (2019). A proposal to study the links between the sociocultural and the linguistic dimensions of eTandem interactions. In A. Turula, M. Kurek & T. Lewis (Eds), *Telecollaboration and virtual exchange across disciplines: in service of social inclusion and global citizenship* (pp. 99-104). Research-publishing.net. https://doi.org/10.14705/rpnet.2019.35.945

grounded claims in respect of their impact on the development of language, intercultural, digital, and/or pedagogical skills. This is linked to the fact that on an epistemological and methodological level, research suffers from a dichotomy between cognitive and sociocultural approaches, which has characterised the literature on telecollaboration, and more widely on second language acquisition thus far (Hulstijn, Young, Ortega, & Bigelow, 2014; Zuengler & Miller, 2006).

On the one hand, the so called 'cognitivist paradigm' is based on the input-interaction framework and the interaction hypothesis (Gass, 1997). This paradigm identified interactional dynamics that are present in any pedagogical environment. It focussed on categories of analysis to develop quantitative studies that allow statistical comparisons between environments. However, this paradigm does not consider the social dimension of learning and it usually ignores the role of the digital environment and of multimodality. When it does, it is within an analytical and experimental epistemology, where different factors are identified as variables and manipulated to study the impact of the presence/absence of an element on (language) acquisition. Such a procedure does not consider, as dynamic complex systems theory suggests (Larsen-Freeman & Cameron, 2008), that the characteristics of an ensemble, a system, are different from the sum of the characteristics of its elements.

On the other hand, 'sociocultural approaches' allow an in-depth view into the development of language competence within the social environment of learners (Lantolf & Thorne, 2006) and consider the relationship between learners and the physical and/or digital environments. However, these studies are almost exclusively case studies and their results are difficult to generalise. Comparison of telecollaborative projects is also quite rare within this paradigm, which hinders the contrastive identification of the outcomes of different models of telecollaboration (O'Dowd, 2018).

The aim of this paper is to suggest a methodological framework proposing categories of analysis that are both relevant for quantitative analysis and anchored to the social and linguistic dimensions of eTandem exchanges.

2. The sociocultural dimension

(Applied) linguists have taken concepts and tools from ethnomethodology and conversation analysis to study verbal interaction. For instance, Mondada (1999) developed a broad ethnomethodological framework to study how interlocutors categorise themselves as well as the activities they are accomplishing through linguistic and paralinguistic means. Following Mondada (1999), an earlier empirical study charted the discursive positionings that eTandem partners adopt during their online conversations (Cappellini & Rivens Mompean, 2013). The main topics of discussion are personal and cultural, defined in an emic perspective. Cultural topics, within this perspective, are usually defined in relation to national cultures[2], while personal topics refer to socialising, hobbies, and daily life. For cultural topics, the following positionings were found (Cappellini & Rivens Mompean, 2013):

- **expert-novice**: this is the most common positioning. The student who talks about the nation where s/he is born positions as the person who has knowledge about it and the interlocutor as the person who has no knowledge and wants to acquire it;

- **expert-expert agreeing**: both interlocutors contribute some knowledge about the topic discussed and the information provided is not in contradiction;

- **expert-expert disagreeing**: both interlocutors contribute some knowledge about the topic at issue and the information provided is contradictory; and

- **novice-novice**: neither interlocutor has the piece of information needed.

These categories cover the possibilities of co-construction of expertise about sociocultural topics within the conversation from an emic point of view. The

---

2. For the serious issues this raises from an intercultural education perspective, see Dervin (2017) from a general point of view and Cappellini and Rivens Mompean (2013) for eTandem more specifically.

model also provides flexibility, since these are open categories in terms of the ethnomethodological procedures carried out to perform these positionings. This two-layered approach to the sociocultural dimension makes possible the openness necessary to describe social practices of co-construction of positioning, while providing the stability necessary to generalise the categorisation of these, therefore allowing comparison among pairs within an eTandem project, or across eTandem projects.

3. The linguistic dimension

To study the linguistic dimension, I drew on the francophone acquisitionist literature (Pekarek Doehler, 2000), which relates concepts from sociocultural theory to conversation analysis. More precisely, I adapted four categories of conversational side sequences from the literature (Cappellini, 2016):

- **potential acquisition of vocabulary**: the learner has a gap in their vocabulary and asks their interlocutor for assistance;

- **potential acquisition of syntax**: the learner has a gap in their understanding of morpho-syntactic issues and asks their interlocutor for assistance;

- **normative evaluation**: the learner produces an utterance containing what the interlocutor considers a mistake, which leads the interlocutor to 'correct' the learner, usually interrupting them; and

- **explicative conversational sequence**: the learner does not understand something the interlocutor says and asks for help.

From the point of view of sociocultural theory (Lantolf & Thorne, 2006), side sequences such as those described above may be a sign of the internalisation of language. The conversational accomplishment of these categories can vary and actual ethnomethodological procedures can provide borderline cases. However, these cases are still categorisable in one of the four broad categories (Cappellini & Pescheux, 2015), therefore allowing statistical analysis.

4. Building complex configurations

The elements presented in the two previous sections can be seen as interconnected from a conversational point of view. In other words, to consider the linguistic dimension through the lens of conversational side sequences allows study of where these side sequences appear during broader conversational sequences characterised in terms of conversational positioning related to the sociocultural dimension.

Combining the category sets (personal topics + the four cultural positionings and the four side sequences) and multiplying them for the two languages of an eTandem and for the two parts of the eTandem session results in 80 possible complex categories. An example of a complex category would be a normative evaluative side sequence for French language appearing during an expert-novice exchange about Chinese culture during the French part of the conversation. The number of occurrences of each complex category can be an indicator of the characteristics of an eTandem conversation, of the conversations of an eTandem pair, of an eTandem setting, or to allow comparisons.

5. Future directions

This proposal has two major limits. The first is that the framework does not take into account the digital dimension. The second is that it is based on research on eTandem conversations, which means that, in other models, other positioning categories could emerge. This is why one of the future directions I intend to explore is to compare the interactions within different telecollaborative models, as was done for Normative Evaluation side sequences in Cappellini and Azaoui (2017). Another future direction will be to use this framework as a tool to study the effects of task implementation on the eTandem interactions.

References

Cappellini, M. (2016). Roles and scaffolding in teletandem interactions – a study of the relations between the sociocultural and the language learning dimensions in a French-Chinese teletandem. *Innovation in Language Learning and Teaching, 10*(1), 6-20. https://doi.org/10.1080/17501229.2016.1134859

Cappellini, M., & Azaoui, B. (2017). Sequences of normative evaluation in two telecollaboration projects: a comparative study of multimodal feedback through desktop videoconference. *Language Learning in Higher Education, 7*(1), 55-80. https://doi.org/10.1515/cercles-2017-0002

Cappellini, M., & Pescheux, M. (2015). La gestion des normes langagières dans un tandem franco-chinois par visioconférence. *Bulletin Suisse de Linguistique Appliquée VALS/ASLA, special issue, 3*, 171-187.

Cappellini, M., & Rivens Mompean, A. (2013). Positionnements culturels dans un tandem sino-fançais par visioconférence. *Sinergies Chine, 8*, 137-149.

Dervin, F. (2017). *Compétences interculturelles*. Editions des Archives Contemporains.

Gass, S. M. (1997). *Input, interaction, and the second language learner*. Routledge.

Hulstijn, J. H., Young, R. F., Ortega, L., & Bigelow, M. (2014). Bridging the gap: cognitive and social approaches to research in second language learning and teaching. *Studies in Second Language Acquisition, 36*(3), 361-421. https://doi.org/10.1017/S0272263114000035

Lantolf, J. P., & Thorne, S. L. (2006). *Sociocultural theory and the genesis of second language development*. Oxford University Press.

Larsen-Freeman, D., & Cameron, L. (2008). *Complex systems and applied linguistics*. Oxford University Press.

Mondada, L. (1999). L'accomplissement de l'étrangéité dans et par l'interaction : procédures de catégorisation des locuteurs. *Langages, 134*, 20-34. https://doi.org/10.3406/lgge.1999.2190

O'Dowd, R. (2018). From telecollaboration to virtual exchange. *Journal of Virtual Exchange, 1*, 1-23. https://doi.org/10.14705/rpnet.2018.jve.1

Pekarek Doehler, S. (Ed.). (2000). *Approches interactionnistes de l'acquisition des langues étrangères. Aile, 12*.

Zuengler, J., & Miller, E. R. (2006). Cognitive and sociocultural perspectives: two parallel SLA worlds? *Tesol Quarterly, 40*(1), 35-58. https://doi.org/10.2307/40264510

13 Lived experience of connected practice: Clavier

Teresa Mackinnon[1]

Abstract

Actors in a large scale Online Intercultural Exchange (OIE) (O'Dowd, 2016) known as Clavier (MacKinnon, 2016) took time to reflect on their personal experiences of an OIE Network (OIEN) through creating auto ethnographic accounts (Nunan & Choi, 2010). Data reflect different contexts, roles and identities. The data were analysed using a grounded theory method to explore the various perspectives, convergences, and divergences. Through this analysis, "[t]he researcher creates an explication, organisation and presentation *of* the data rather than discovering order *within* the data. The discovery process consists of discovering the ideas the *researcher* has about the data after interacting with it" (Charmaz, 1990, p. 1169, cited in Willig, 2013, p. 77, emphasis in original). This 'discovery process' was followed by a series of online discussions where we grappled with the question of how best to present this complex picture with its many facets given the short period of presentation time in the conference. An account emerged of the transformative nature of connected practice. The process of preparing this performance for the UNICollaboration conference in Krakow took the actors to a new point in their professional lives.

Keywords: connected practice, complexity, impact, co-creation.

---

1. University of Warwick, Coventry, England; t.mackinnon@warwick.ac.uk

How to cite this chapter: Mackinnon, T. (2019). Lived experience of connected practice: Clavier. In A. Turula, M. Kurek & T. Lewis (Eds), *Telecollaboration and virtual exchange across disciplines: in service of social inclusion and global citizenship* (pp. 105-110). Research-publishing.net. https://doi.org/10.14705/rpnet.2019.35.946

© 2019 Teresa Mackinnon (CC BY)

1. Introduction

Communicating the various perspectives of practitioners who have designed and delivered a large-scale virtual exchange in their various contexts over several years to an audience who may be unfamiliar with the subject matter within a short presentation could be confusing and ultimately fail to achieve our objectives. The presentation was to combine our analysis with visualisations produced as a result of open interactions through social media, sharing insights into the factors that have contributed to the richness and challenges of connected practice and how this can forge professional identities through the relationships within a network. The constraints of time and place, the richness of the story we had to tell led to a decision to turn the presentation into a performance. We decided that if our audience were to understand the transformative nature of our lived experience, we would need to involve them in an unexpected event which would allow a real insight into the nature of virtual exchanges. Here I will explain the process of collaborative script writing and share the product we co-created.

2. Methodology

The 'discovery process' used by the practitioners, as described in the abstract, was the first step to uncover how each of us perceived our lived experience of implementing virtual exchange. Our aim was to arrive at a deeper shared understanding arising from reading each other's individual auto ethnographic accounts, which we published online and shared through Google Docs. These accounts were encoded for synergies and points of divergence using a system devised by each individual practitioner in order to allow for individual meaning making. The terminology used by each practitioner to thematically describe their perceptions of the accounts was then the focus of our online discussions and informed our decision making when creating the script for our performance. Aware of the importance of conveying a clear understanding of what it meant to live through a virtual exchange, we agreed to use a multimedia approach to communicating the experience. Clavier's virtual exchange tasks were multimodal, these were compiled onto a Padlet board – a virtual notice board –

so that audience members and those outside the conference could explore and comment on them. We started to script our performance in order to place our audience in the midst of some of the lived experiences of Clavier, offering them an opportunity to witness first hand some of the challenges, frustrations, and epiphanies experienced to create space for them to draw their own conclusions about the nature of virtual exchange and the impact it has on one's physical existence. The script was accompanied by a set of slides including video clips and images which presented visual metaphors to support the concepts emerging from the data analysis. Our performance space was a university classroom with a data projector, screen, and conventional seating.

3. Results

The auto ethnographies and further information about the practitioners revealed different interpretations and experiences as seen in Table 1 below.

Table 1. Auto ethnographies

Teresa	Institutional profile[2]	Stories of connection : http://teresa-nextsteps.blogspot.co.uk/2017/11/stories-of-connection.html
		More stories of connection: http://teresa-nextsteps.blogspot.co.uk/2017/11/more-stories-of-connection.html
Marcin	Institutional profile[3]	https://tinyurl.com/y7zzhho6
Claude	Institutional profile[4]	https://tinyurl.com/y9av5pk7
Simon	Institutional profile[5]	http://tachesdesens.blogspot.co.uk/2018/02/what-shines-out.html
		http://tachesdesens.blogspot.co.uk/2018/02/defining-clavier_11.html

2. https://warwick.ac.uk/fac/arts/modernlanguages/academic/teresa-mackinnon/
3. http://www.ifa.filg.uj.edu.pl/marcin-kleban
4. https://warwick.ac.uk/fac/arts/modernlanguages/academic/claude-tregoat/
5. http://lrl.uca.fr/rubrique46.html

Chapter 13

The encoding produced the following shown in Table 2.

Table 2.   Encoding the data

Teresa	https://tinyurl.com/y94tq37t
Simon	https://tinyurl.com/yaaugf5l
Claude	https://tinyurl.com/y8xfxvg5

The script planning was undertaken using a negotiated framework built upon the themes that had emerged from the auto ethnographies:

- spaces, identities, and affinities,
- unpredictable growth,
- gardening – teacher roles, and
- connections and mutations,

The script emerged through discussing each of these themes as encoded during the discovery process in order to unpack the meaning making each of us had thematically identified and defining ways to make our audience experience them and draw their own conclusions. This sociocultural approach (Vygotsky, 1998) was adopted in order to communicate our professional development through the virtual exchange to others in a way that they could also be impacted (Shabani, 2016). The resultant slides present three phases that incorporated the themes above:

- spaces, identities,
- nature, nurture, network, and
- criss-crossing.

The collaborative script writing experience was a lively one. It was carried out through several online synchronous meetings and shared Google Docs. It consisted of a debate on the terminology used in the encoding process towards a shared conceptualisation of the results of our earlier data analysis. The resultant script is available in the annex and includes references to slide numbers and multimedia as it was shown during the performance.

The last words should be left to those who experienced the performance. Feedback from audience members surveyed anonymously online after the event described the performance as "thought provoking" and "interesting". It would appear that the performance was sufficiently challenging to provoke reflection. When asked to reflect on the experience, the responses showed audience members had engaged in the sense making we had hoped for:

> "Confusing at first even if I realised that it was a role play and was a little sceptical to the style. As it progressed I began to accept the format and found the latter stages very interesting".

> "The presentation was puzzling at the beginning as I did not expect the presentation to be in such a different/theatrical format… However, the format was particularly effective in conveying the 'lived experience' and thus perfectly matched the aim of this presentation".

4. Conclusions

The most important aspects of our understanding of the lived experience of OIE reveal similarities with understanding our physical existence and agency in the real world. Understanding of context, situatedness, and identity matter to our ability to connect with others effectively. In the virtual world, this includes the digital skills to manage our presence. The willingness to be open to the ideas of others and to review our role as a teacher or a learner can speed progress and innovation. A commitment to experiment and reflect both alone and with others provides fertile ground for network growth. It would appear that, as in life itself, resilience and positivity contribute to overcoming the many barriers we face.

The script writing process drew on the various strengths of the Clavier team. It combined the digital creativity which had featured throughout the Clavier virtual exchange with the metaphors and reflections of the actors involved. The process of reflecting on our own experiences, followed by reading and analysing each other's reflections, and then coming together in order to co-create and perform a play took us all beyond our comfort zones. However, collaborating over the past seven years in the Clavier project had familiarised us with the skills and qualities needed to achieve a shared goal. The mutual respect and trust which had been nurtured over that time made the shared creative process possible. Co-creation is the most complex and demanding of telecollaborative activities (O'Dowd & Ware, 2009), and in committing to this participation at the conference we had proven to ourselves how professionally transformative the virtual exchange experience had been for us all.

References

Charmaz, K. (1990). "Discovering" chronic illness: using grounded theory. *Social Science and Medicine, 30*(11), 1161-1172.

MacKinnon, T. (2016). The Clavier network. In R. O'Dowd & T. Lewis (Eds), *Online intercultural exchange: policy, pedagogy, practice* (pp. 235-240). Routledge.

Nunan, D., & Choi, J. (Eds). (2010). *Language and culture: reflective narratives and the emergence of identity*. Routledge. https://doi.org/10.4324/9780203856987

O'Dowd, R. (2016). Emerging trends and new directions in telecollaborative learning. *CALICO Journal, 33*(3), 291-310. https://doi.org/10.1558/cj.v33i3.30747

O'Dowd, R., & Ware, P. (2009). Critical issues in telecollaborative task design. *Computer Assisted Language Learning, 22*(2), 173-188. https://doi.org/10.1080/09588220902778369

Shabani, K. (2016). Applications of Vygotsky's sociocultural approach for teachers' professional development. *Cogent Education*. https://doi.org/10.1080/2331186X.2016.1252177

Vygotsky, L. S. (1998). Infancy (M. Hall, Trans.). In R. W. Rieber (Ed.), *The collected works of L. S. Vygotsky: Vol. 5. Child psychology* (pp. 207-241). Plenum Press.

Willig, C. (2013). *Introducing qualitative research in psychology*. McGraw-Hill.

14. Vocabulary learning in Mandarin Chinese – German eTandems

Julia Renner[1]

Abstract

This article deals with vocabulary learning in synchronous, multimodal eTandems focussing on Mandarin Chinese as a target language. In doing so, the study adopts an emic, conversation analytic perspective and triangulates self-reported data from learner diaries with recordings of actual eTandem conversations. The analysis of the learner diaries showed that the participants perceive to have mostly improved their vocabulary. In order to identify the video extracts for qualitative analysis, the vocabulary items mentioned in the learner diaries were located within the interactions and analysed by means of Conversation Analysis (CA). For the most part, the analysed sequences classify as instances of word searches during which a clear preference for self-initiated collaborative repair was observed. Peer-assistance of the expert speaker was only performed on request of the learner. Furthermore, the multimodal setting shows how the participant's gaze plays a key-role in assessing the status of the word search.

Keywords: multimodal eTandems, conversation analysis, vocabulary learning, word searches.

---

1. University of Vienna, Vienna, Austria; julia.renner@univie.ac.at

How to cite this chapter: Renner, J. (2019). Vocabulary learning in Mandarin Chinese – German eTandems. In A. Turula, M. Kurek & T. Lewis (Eds), *Telecollaboration and virtual exchange across disciplines: in service of social inclusion and global citizenship* (pp. 111-118). Research-publishing.net. https://doi.org/10.14705/rpnet.2019.35.947

Chapter 14

1. Introduction: CA-for-eTandem language learning research

CA is a research approach that centres around the question of how people manage talk-in-interaction. In the field of language learning and teaching research, CA is recognised as a method to investigate learner interaction since it may "document in a way that, for example, main-stream [second language acquisition] studies cannot, what students are doing when they are engaged in a learning activity, and what they are doing at a later stage when they have [...] learned to become accomplished users of certain linguistic resources in interaction" (Gardner, 2013, p. 609).

Research on synchronous, multimodal eTandems has only recently started to focus on interactional dimensions from a CA point of view. Existing studies cover topics such as role taking and scaffolding (Cappellini, 2016), thematic development (Black, 2017), and repair (El-Hariri & Renner, 2017). The current study falls into this line of research, while putting a particular emphasis on the multimodal nature of eTandem interactions. Adopting an emic perspective, the current study poses two research questions:

- What do the Mandarin Chinese learners perceive to have learnt during the eTandem sessions?

- How is this learning interactively realised within the conversations?

2. Project outline

Altogether, six Mandarin Chinese/German dyads participated in the eTandem initiative of the current study. The Mandarin Chinese learners were students or graduates of the 'Chinese Studies' programme at the University of Vienna in Austria; the German learners were students of 'German Studies' at the National Kaohsiung First University of Science and Technology in Taiwan. The main objective of the project was to promote oral interaction in real-time, therefore the participants communicated with each other through video-conferencing tools such as ooVoo or Skype. To facilitate communication, a list of possible communication topics (e.g. 'hobbies', 'travelling', 'future plans', etc.) was provided by the organisers, however, the participants were strongly encouraged to develop their own topics. Since the initiative was created as an outer-curricular activity, the interactions took place outside the regular language courses and students were free to choose the time and location of their sessions. Regarding the research agenda of the project, the participants were explicitly involved in the process of data collection. They were encouraged to provide as much data as possible, but decided on their own terms what they wanted to submit to the researcher. To ensure full transparency, all participants were informed about the research goals and methodology beforehand.

3. Methodology

The current study triangulates self-reported data from learner diaries with interactional data from the actual eTandem-sessions. The learner diaries were semi-structured and consisted of three blocks: (1) 'General thoughts about today's session', (2) 'My learning process', and (3) 'My tandem partner's role'. Each block included up to three open-ended statements (e.g. 'In today's session I have learnt...') that the participants were asked to complete. For the purpose of the current study, the second block has been selected as a basis for the analysis.

Interactional data from the eTandem-sessions were obtained by recordings through ooVoo itself or an additional desktop recording programme for those who chose Skype, as well as by copies of the text-chat scripts. The final data corpus (Table 1) consists of 29 hours and 33 minutes of audio/video recordings with corresponding text-chat scripts, 28 learner diaries (Chinese learners), and 17 tutoring reflections (Taiwanese tandem partners).

The current study proceeded with a two-step analysis: firstly, the learner diaries were analysed to understand what the learners perceive to have learnt during the eTandem sessions; and secondly, specific items listed in the learner diaries were located within the interactions and examined from a conversation analytic perspective.

Table 1. Overview of the data corpus

Dyad	Recordings	Learner diaries	Tutoring reflections
eTandem 1	6 (altogether 6h 29 min.)	7	5
eTandem 2	5 (altogether 4h 27 min.)	3	0
eTandem 3	5 (altogether 5h 24 min.)	5	5
eTandem 4	4 (altogether 4 h 30 min.)	4	5
eTandem 5	5 (altogether 5 h 07 min.)	3	2
eTandem 6	4 (altogether 3 h 36 min.)	4	0

4. Results

The analysis of the learner diaries showed that learners perceive to have improved in three domains: (1) language-related aspects, (2) content-related aspects, and (3) technical aspects. For the purpose of the current study, language-related aspects have been examined more closely. Most entries were concerned with vocabulary learning (10 entries), followed by formulaic expressions on phrasal and sentence level (5 entries) and function words (3 entries). The individual entries varied in their specificity – some were written in a more general manner, some mentioned specific items. From the latter, a total of 41 listed vocabulary items were located within the interactions and sequentially analysed. Except for one, all sequences were negotiations that could be described as sequences of word searches (altogether 30 instances; 25 instances within the learners' speech, and five instances within the tandem partners' speech), language-related feedback (six instances), non-understandings (three instances), and one metalinguistic reflection. The analysis of the interactional data revealed that word searches by the learners were indicated verbally through syllable stretches, repetitions, pauses, re-starts, and perturbation signals, and non-verbally through a gaze-shift away from the camera/screen and/or a distinct thinking-face. During that stage, the tandem partners did not interfere in the process of the word search yet. From the perspective of the tandem partners, non-verbal cues, in particular the direction of their interlocutor's gaze, seemed to play an important role in assessing whether a co-participation in the word search process is solicited or not. The following two transcripts exemplify this argument.

Extract 1 in Figure 1 shows an unproblematic, straightforward sequence of a collaborative word search activity. E's (Chinese learner) speech in Line 1 starts out in Mandarin Chinese and is characterised by non-lexical perturbations, followed by a longer pause. He then switches to German and articulates a word while shifting his gaze away. After a short pause he repeats the same word with a rising intonation while re-focussing his gaze towards the recipient. L (Taiwanese tandem partner) interprets E's code-switched utterance with a rising intonation, combined with a gaze shift towards her/the camera as a clear invitation to participate in the word search, as her contribution in Line 2 shows.

Figure 1. Extract 1

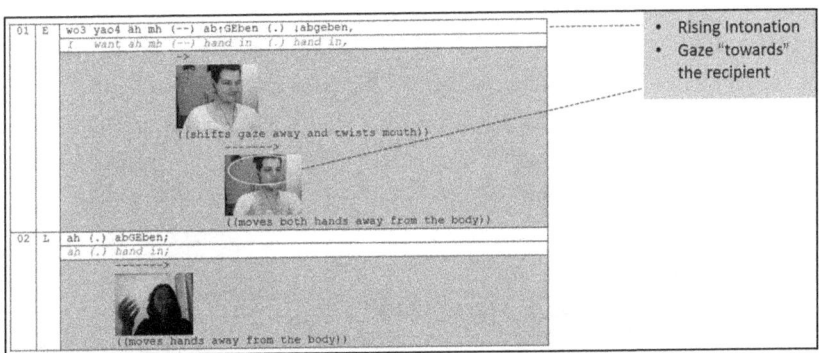

The beginning of Extract 2 (Figure 2, Line 8) shows how H (Chinese learner) articulates an explicit request for help (how do you say) while at the same time shifting her gaze away from the interlocutor/the camera. Even though the request for help is verbalised more explicitly (direct question) than in Extract 1, the tandem partner remains silent here (Lines 9-12). In comparison to Extract 1, the crucial difference here is that H's gaze is not focussed on the interlocutor/the

Chapter 14

camera during her verbalised invitation to the word search; the verbal and non-verbal behaviour of H are giving off conflicting cues. The analysis of this extract therefore arrives at the conclusion that, at least for this example, the non-verbal cues override the verbal cues.

Figure 2.   Extract 2

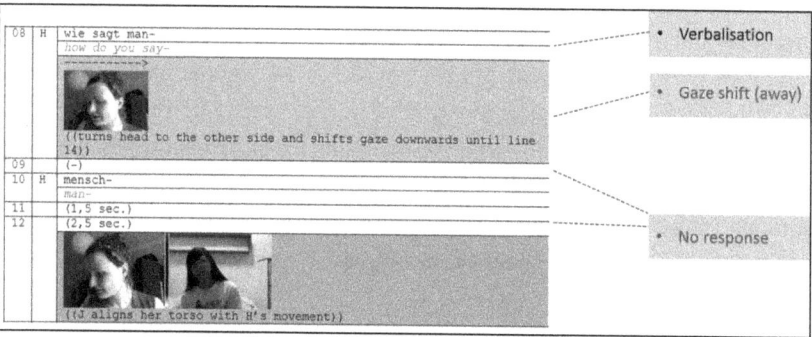

These conflicting cues lead to a very delayed response of J (Taiwanese tandem partner, Line 13), which is not taken up by H, but followed by a distinct pause (2 seconds) (Figure 3, Line 14). To clarify the argument being made here, it is important to note that H's gaze is still not focussed towards the interlocutor/the camera at that time. Only during the last 0.5 seconds of the pause in Line 14 does H re-focus her gaze and asks for repetition (Line 16). In Line 17, J responds again, which finally leads to a solution of the word search (not shown in Extract 3).

Figure 3.   Extract 3

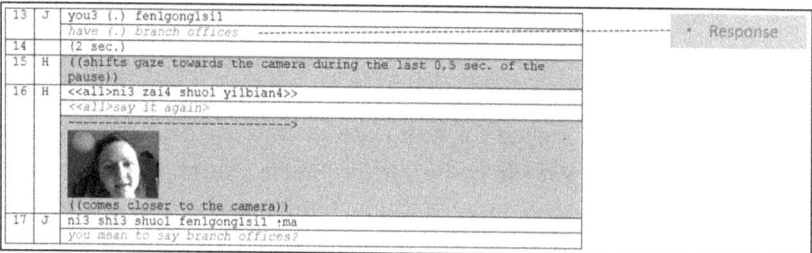

5. Discussion and conclusion

The literature shows that gaze seems to play a key role in regulating the invitation to the recipient(s) to the word search, assessing its status, and to what extent a co-participation is perceived to be solicited (Goodwin & Goodwin, 1986). Critics of Goodwin and Goodwin's (1986) position, such as Rossano (2013), claim that "no systematic evidence for this claim is presented and [...] this apparent solicitation through gaze is, in fact, unsuccessful" (p. 316). The current study shows that in this context, the occurrence of a recipient-focussed gaze seems clear to the recipient, while the absence of it causes trouble. The results therefore correspond with the findings of Goodwin and Goodwin (1986). All analysed sequences of successful word searches shared the common feature that a favourable environment for co-participation was created by the learner (verbalised, through intonation and facial expressions) before the tandem partner interfered. Previous research on word searches (Brouwer, 2003) in non-native/ expert speaker interaction defined the solicited co-participation of the expert speaker as one of the crucial aspects that turn word searches into language learning opportunities. The current study supports these findings for language learning in an eTandem context.

References

Black, E. (2017). Extending talk on a prescribed discussion topic in a learner-native speaker eTandem learning task. *Language Learning in Higher Education, 7*(1), 161-184. https://doi.org/10.1515/cercles-2017-0005

Brouwer, C. (2003). Word Searches in NNS–NS Interaction: Opportunities for Language Learning? *Modern Language Journal, 87,* iv, 534-545. https://doi.org/10.1111/1540-4781.00206

Cappellini, M. (2016). Roles and scaffolding in teletandem interactions: a study of the relations between the sociocultural and the language learning dimensions in a French–Chinese teletandem. *Innovation in Language Learning and Teaching, 10*(1), 6-20. https://doi.org/10.1080/17501229.2016.1134859

El-Hariri, Y., & Renner, J. (2017). Non-understanding in eTandem conversations. In H. Funk, M. Gerlach & D. Spaniel-Weise (Eds), *Handbook for foreign language learning in online tandems and educational settings* (pp. 122-140). Peter Lang.

Gardner, R. (2013). Conversation analysis and orientation to learning. In J. Sidnell & T. Stivers (Eds), *The handbook of conversation analysis* (pp. 593-612). Blackwell-Wiley.

Goodwin, M. H., & Goodwin, C. (1986). Gesture and coparticipation in the activity of searching for a word. *Semiotica, 62*(1/2), 51-75.

Rossano, F. (2013). Emotion, affect and conversation. In J. Sidnell & T. Stivers (Eds), *The handbook of conversation analysis* (pp. 330-350). Blackwell-Wiley.

Author index

A
Albá Duran, Juan viii, 3, 31
Austin, Todd vii, 3, 57

B
Barbier, Régine viii, 2, 23
Benjamin, Elizabeth viii, 2, 23

C
Caluianu, Daniela viii, 2, 7
Cappellini, Marco ix, 5, 99
Cavalari, Suzi Marques Spatti ix, 4, 73
Creelman, Alastair ix, 2, 15

G
Giralt, Marta ix, 4, 65

K
Knysh, Alexander x, 3, 57
Kurek, Malgorzata v, 1

L
Lewis, Tim v, 1
Lindner, Rachel x, 4, 81
Lochner, Johanna x, 3, 41
Löwe, Corina x, 2, 15

M
Mackinnon, Teresa xi, 5, 105
Marchewka, Małgorzata xi, 3, 49
Matochkina, Anna xi, 3, 57
Meechan, Philomena xi, 3, 57
Murray, Liam xii, 4, 65

O
O'Brien, Dónal xii, 4, 81
Oggel, Gerdientje xii, 3, 31

R
Raina, Reeta xiii, 3, 49
Renner, Julia xiii, 5, 111

S
Štefl, Martin xiii, 4, 91

T
Turula, Anna v, 1

U
Ulanova, Daria xiii, 3, 57

www.ingramcontent.com/pod-product-compliance
Lightning Source LLC
Chambersburg PA
CBHW031633160426
43196CB00006B/403